MONEY SHALL BE YOUR SLAVE

KINGSLEY UDOKA NWACHUKWU

ISBN:
978-978-792-442-6

PUBLISHED BY

KINGSLEY UDOKA NWACHUKWU
No. 17, Remson Primary School Emordi Street, by Chemist B/stop, / Alaba Int'l., Ojo Lagos, Nigeria.
Email: pastorkingsleymissions@gmail.com
Tel: 08038764072, 08081031917

TABLE OF CONTENT

INTRODUCTION

DEDICATION

CHAPTER 1

PROPHECY

CHAPTER 2

MY CASE IS DIFFERENT

CHAPTER 3

MENDING DYING HOPE

CHAPTER 4

ABOVE ONLY

CHAPTER 5

RECOVERING THE STARS OF JACOB

CHAPTER 6

COVENS THAT MAKES MEN RICH ARE NOT STRONGER THAN THE ANOINTING

CHAPTER 7

COMING OUT FROM SEVERE POVERTY

CHAPTER 8

BREAKING ANCIENT CURSES OF POVERTY

CHAPTER 9

MAKING MONEY IS A GRACE

CHAPTER 10

THE LIVING WORD IS YOUR SUFFICIENCY

CHAPTER 11

POWER OF THE COVENANT

CHAPTER 12

WISDOM FOR SUPERNATURAL WEALTH

CHAPTER 13

WALKING IN FINANCIAL DOMINION

CHAPTER 14

PRINCIPLES OF SUCCESS FOR BELIEVERS

CHAPTER 15

MIRACLES IN THE FOLD OF FRUSTRATED BUSINESSMEN

CHAPTER 16

MONEY SHALL BE YOUR SLAVE

CHAPTER 17

ANOINTING THAT BREEDS MILLONIARES AND BILLIONAIRES

CHAPTER 18

PURPOSE OF SUPERNATURAL FAVOUR

CHAPTER 19

OPENING THE REALMS OF POSSIBILITIES

CHAPTER 20

GOD IS SIGNING MANY CHEQUE BOOKS

CHAPTER 21

IT SHALL BE LIKE A DREAM

CHAPTER 22

PRAYER WORKS FINANCIAL MIRACLES

INTRODUCTION

Let God be glorified for his word endureth forever, and let the word of God be magnified among the believers in the church of Jesus Christ.

There is a move of God in the affairs of the saint ordained to confirm the covenant of God among the people of God this end-time in such a way that the promise of God for the church will have preeminence and prevail in the lives of the faithful ones in the household of God in this dispensation.

Child of God, one of the covenant of God that will be confirmed in the body of Christ in this generation is to restore financial dominion to the saints of God in every field of human endeavours.

Financial dominion of the saints is a covenant that cannot fail to come to pass, in the affairs of God's people, neither can it be manipulated not to have clear manifestation with open testimonies among those that believe in our Lord Jesus Christ.

Friends, financial dominion is a supernatural right of every believer that empowers you not to be a slave to money, because by the virtue of the covenant money is ordained to be your slave, in such a way that it will be obvious that you are walking in the manifold sufficiency and abundance of supernatural blessings, prosperity, success, riches, wealth, provisions and supplies in your financial life as a believer.

*"Money shall be your slave "*is a book inspired by the Holy Spirit to re-arrange the financial position, status, and portion of the believers in the economic system of nations so as to give the saints upper hand to control wealth and riches as their inheritance in Christ this end-time in the economy of the nations.

By the grace of God, as you read this book titled *"Money Shall Be Your Slave"* the Holy Spirit shall take you into the realm of revelation where you shall encounter faith, insight, light, truth, rhema word that will quicken your understanding to tap into the supernatural wealth that will yield the fruits of practical testimonies in your financial life as a Christian in the name of Jesus Christ.

DEDICATION

This book is dedicated to the righteousness of God, and to the faithfulness of God to his covenant with his people in the name of God the Father, the Son and the Holy Ghost.

CHAPTER 1

PROPHECY

When a prophet is sent with the word of the Lord to the people, they will be a prophecy that will reveal the work of God, and the purpose of God to people's economy in every issues of life that is troubling the saints.

When a prophet is sent to prophesy to the people, it means that divine visitation has taken place in the camp of God's people.Light is about to shine in your path that will destroy the gangup of powers of darkness against welfare of the saints.

Prophecy is a word of the Lord handed over to a prophet by God as an oracle that is being sent to God's people to reveal the will of God for the children of God in the moment of confusion, frustration, and defeat in any issues of life.

"I will hear what God the Lord will speak;
For he will speak peace unto his people, and to
His saints, but let them not turn again to folly".

Psalm 85:8

There is a ringing bell from heaven sounding like a trumpet in the affairs of the saints of God on earth, and God told me that the hour ordained for the believers to enter into the realm of financial dominion globally has come, and it shall be done in a moment to equip the church with wealth and riches that is prepared to preach the gospel of Christ around the world before the second coming of Jesus Christ.

As I was in the Spirit celebrating this goodness, the Spirit of God gave me an oracle to declare it boldly to the covenant people of God that the dispensation that money shall submit to be the slaves of the faithful ones in the body of Christ is around the corner, and it shall come to pass in a moment.

"The eyes of your understanding being enlightened;
That ye may know what is the hope of his calling,
And what the riches of the glory of his inheritance in the saints.
And what is the exceeding greatness of his power to us ward who believe,

According to the working of his mighty power which he wrought in Christ, when he raised him from the dead, and set him at his own right Hand in heavenly places. And hath put all things under his feet, And gave him to be the head over all things to the church.

Ephesians 1:18-20, 22

The power that subjected all things under the feet of Christ is the power of God, and for the biblical prophecies concerning covenant wealth to be fulfilled among the saints in this end-time, shall be subjected to be the slave that will save the saints of God

The power that made Jesus Christ the head over all things to the church is the power of God, and that same power is ordained to confirm the covenant of supernatural prosperity among the saints by giving the church of Jesus Christ the controlling power over money, market system, business realm, and economy affairs of this world.

Based on this clear revelation, it means that one of the prophecy that is yet to have complete fulfillment in the reign of the saints, and the church in the affairs of nations is the subjection of money to become the portion, inheritance, and the possession of the believers as a gift of wealth and riches that they recieved from God for the service of God's kingdom and for the advancement of the gospel.

Friend, I was sent as a prophet of goodnews, and I am standing on the mountain of God to announce to you that the supernatural is set to play a role in your financial matters, and this same occurrence will break the siege of financial crises, financial losses, financial struggles, and the yoke of poverty in your life, and business without delay.

"Who hath declared from the beginning,
That we may know? And before time, that we may say,
He is righteous? Yea, there is none that sheweth, yea, there is
None that delcareth, yea, there is none
That heareth your words.
The first shall say to Zion, behold, behold them; and I will give to Jerusalem
One that bringeth good tidings.

Isaiah 41:26-27

I am a good-news bearer set on the mountain of the Lord to declare to you that the miraculous has laid their hands upon your financial problems, and as a result of this divine visitation, the saints of God are about to enter into the fullness of financial dominion where money shall serve the believers,in realities in the name of our Lord Jesus Christ.

CHAPTER 2
MY CASE IS DIFFERENT

My case is different simply means that as a child of God you are empowered by the virtue of salvation and redemption that Christ brought to you to enjoy covenant exemptions that forbids calamity to befall me in the midst of the people, even when it is happening to others.

My case is different simply means that according to your profession of faith as a child of God, you are binded by the covenant to walk in the positive experience, positive story, positive results, and positive encounters in the issues of life when other people are experiencing life in the negative.

"Thy way, O God, is in the sanctuary,
Who is so great a God as our God. Thou hast with thine arm
Redeemed thy people, the sons of Jacob and Joseph.
The waters saw thee, O God, the waters saw thee, they were afraid,
The depths also were troubled.
The clouds poured out waters, the skies sent out a sound,
Thine arrows also went abroad.

Psalm 77:13-17

The ways of God are the ways of the supernatural, and the miraculous ordained to bring you into a supernatural encounter with a different life experience at a time when the people are victims of circumstances in life issues.

By the virtue of being a child of God, you must believe that your case is different in every situation for that is the way to activate faith, confession, declaration, and the decree of your tongue to believe God that possibilities is your reality at a time when the people are being held bound by impossibilities.

As a covenant child of God, the realm where you live is the realm of possibilities, and a world where everything that is happening in your life is being regulated by the integrity of God's word.The word of God has total control over the affairs of man, and life issues that you are going through on a daily basis.

Friend, my case is different simply means accepting what God says concerning you and to believe what the word of God declared concerning you in the daily life experience with total faith on the integrity of God's word to confirm the promises of God upon your situations in the midst of challenges.

"I am the LORD thy God which brought thee out of the land of Egypt Open thy mouth wide, and I will fill it.

Psalm 81:10

In the kingdom of God you need to understand that faith answers to what your declare, and realities answers to what you believe, light answers to what you know, but miracles answers to what you do with what you proclaim.

Based on this understanding, it means to believe that your case is different as a child of God is not where the miracle lies, rather the miracles lies in what you do with what you believe in your walk with God.

My case is different is a prophetic declaration that gives you knowledge to walk in the light of God's promises for you in a contrary situation for that is the verdict of God in his word for your life as a believer in the Lord Jesus Christ.

For example, the bible recorded that when the Egyptians were experiencing hardship, bad economy, severe famine in the land, the children of Israel are enjoying plenty, abundance, sufficiency, and surplus in the camp in the land of Goshea.

In the book of Exodus Chapter 1:15-22, Pharaoh gave the mid-wives in Egypt receive the order to kill every male child that were to be born in the camp of Israelites, but in the mist of all that, when it gets to the turn of Moses, the midwives preserved his life.

For instance, Goliath was a giant and mighty warrior, but when it gets to the time when he will kill David, his corpse was laid low. This examples are signs that shows the evil that is befalling others, are not permitted to befall you.

The financial frustration and poverty that is coming to persecute sons of men in the financial system of this world cannot raise it's ugly head against you, because according to the covenant, you are in a dispensation where you have an appointment with God to have money as your slave in your life.

"And they shall be mine, saith the Lord of hosts, In that day when I make up my jewels, and I will spare them,

As a man spareth his own son that serveth him.
Then shall you return and discern between the righteous and the wicked,
Between him that serveth God, and that serveth him not.

Malachi 3:17-18

To believe that your case is different is a faith that professes the verdict of God's word to have expression in your life issues, but the truth remains that what you believe atimes is limited in bringing salvation to you in the contrary situation when it does not lead you to application of faith in the presence of opposing circumstances.

Based on this revelation, permit me to tell you that money shall be your slave, is a promise of God ordained to confirm that your case is different financiallyin the hard times.You should understand that for money to be your slave in realities, your faith must produce knowledge, and knowledge must lead you to the light, and that light must lead you to take a position of responsibility in your walk with God which is able to confirm the integrity of God's word, and the realities of financial covenant to be established in your life as your daily testimonies

CHAPTER 3
MENDING DYING HOPE

Hope is a precious gift of God that empowers faith to deliver your desired expectations from God, Hope is virtue of the spirit that empowers the soul, the spirit, and the mind of a believer to hold unto God's promises, and to have positive mindset until your desires in overwhelming challenges of life becomes a reality.

Child of God, faith cannot work in your life without hope, the word of God cannot yield fruits in your life without hope, and the promises of God cannot produce living testimonies in your life in the absence of hope. Hope is ordain by God to be the anchor that sustains your faith, your walk with God, your confessions, and your prayers till your desires before God becomes a reality.

Now faith Is the substances of things
Hoped for, the evidence of things not seen.

Hebrews 11:1

According to this scripture, hope is the evidence of things not seen, which simply means that hope is a spiritual thing, a virtue of the spirit that gives you assurance of the future, and empowers you with a living and strong convictions that life, events, and the future will surely be a blessing, and cause things to fall in places in your own favour.

Hope is like an anchor that drives life, and existence of man to be positive about the issues of life that things will surely work in your favour even in contradicting, confused, and unpredicted circumstances of life.
Friend, when hope is dead life become meaningless, and your existence will begin to lose value before your very eyes, because you will begin to lose control of your future, your thoughts, and your mindset.

As a man thinketh in his heart
So he is

Proverb 23:7a

The problem that we are facing in this generation, many people are loosing their hope, and when hope is lost the future is lost, the promises of God cannot function in the atmosphere of dead hopes.

The problem we are facing today in the church of Jesus Christ is that many believers have lost their faith, they have lost their future, and as a result of this, their future seems to be shaking because they have lost confidence In the efficacy of God's promises as a result of complicated issues of life that has lasted for a long time.

MENDING DYING HOPE

Child of God, have you lost faith on God's promises you need to renew and activate your hope now because the promises of God standeth sure.

If you have lost your hope about the future to the extent that you are no longer sure of what your tomorrow is going to become, since your today is not treating you with kindness, you need to revive your hope because in the midst of uncertainty, the word of God stands sure.

WHY IS YOUR HOPE FADING AWAY

Why is your hope fading away, why do you choose to allow unpleasant situations and circumstances to destroy your hope about tomorrow, why do you choose to allow afflictions of life to destroy your convictions about the future to the extend that you are losing confidence on the power of God that is able to subdue the negative occurrences in your life, and to establish his better promises concerning you according to the word of God.

For I know the thoughts that I think towards you, saith the Lord, thoughts of peace, and not of evil, to give you an expected end.

Jeremiah 29:11

The thought of God towards you is good, why can't you believe it, and have strong convictions about it. The plan of God for your future is good, why can't you be positive in your thinking about your tomorrow.

The reason why many believers are living in frustration today is because they are losing their confidence on the verdict of God's word, the future is becoming unrealistic to so many people because the circumstance that surrounded their existence, and survival presently is telling them that there is way that their future dreamscan become a reality.

There is glory attached to your future, don't lose it, you have a glorious future in God hold unto it, and have strong assurance in your thinking, your confession, and in your actions that your dreams about tomorrow will surely be a reality, and you will see things changing in your situations.

HOPE IS A PRECIOUS GIFT OF GOD FOR A BELIEVER

Hope is a precious gift of God for a believer, it is hope that empowers your faith to wait upon God until your petitions are answered by God.Hope is all about waiting upon the lord in the midst of unwanted circumstance with strong convictions that believed in God, and that what you believed in the word of God shall surely come to pass in your life.

Hope is a precious gift of God to a believer that empower you to have confidence that promises of God will dominate life issues in your existence, and in your walk with God to establish the counsel of God concerning you as your reality.

Hope is a precious gift of God that empowers you to have a living expectation that your tomorrow is secured irrespective of how insecure that your today may seems to be.

Beloved, when hope start dying in your Christian life, it means that your future is under attack, and if nothing is done by you will discover that your existence as God's creation will begin to lose glory, purpose, and a reason to live.

Hope deferred maketh the heart sick,
But when the desire cometh, it is a tree of life.
Proverb 13:12

Beloved, hold unto hope as a precious gift of God this end-time, you need it to walk in the realm of overcomers and more than conquerors who will see the fulfilment of God's promises in their lives irrespective of opposing circumstances.

The believers this end-time are not going to be men of faith alone, but also men of hope, you need faith to hold unto God to confirm his promises in your life, but hope is holding untoyour future with strong conviction that the dreams of your life most surely come to pass even when the occurrences of the period where you find yourself is telling you that it is not going to be possible.

SIGNS TO SHOW THAT YOUR HOPE IS FADING AWAY AS ACHILD OF GOD

1. **FRUSTRATION**

   it is forbidden for a believer to be frustrated, and it is an abomination for the creation of God to be stranded in life. When hope starts fading away in your life, it is a sign that you have lost your faith in God, which means that the ability to trust God in every situation as a reliable God is no longer working in your life.

   The reason for frustration in the lives of many believers is when they have been beaten, and oppressed by bad events of life for a long time, you will begin to feel that the promises of God has abandoned you, rise up and receive your hope, and come out of that frustration because there is a miracle is about to happen in your life, surely it must come to pass.

2. **TOTAL DISCOURAGEMENT IN LIFE**

   When your hope starts fading away, your courage will start dying, your Christian life will be filled with a lot of discouragement in such a way that you will begin to doubt the promises of God.

   If you are in the state of discouragement right how as a believer I want you to summon courage again to believe in that future that God handed over to you, God is still interested in you, and the hour that he will magnify his promises concerning you above the opposing circumstances of your life has come, and it must surely come to pass.

3. **LOST OF CONFIDENCE**

   When lost of confidence in yourself, in your future, in your dream sets in, it means that you have lost confidence on the promises of God for your life as a believer in the word of God, and that is a clear sign that your hope is fading away.

Man's goings are of the Lord; how can a man then understand his own way?

Proverbs 20:24

Your confidence as a believer is like a light that brightens your future, and causes that future to bow to God's promises for your life. When there is confidence in your life is a sign that faith is potent, and it is a sign that hope is effectual to a point at which impossibilities will give way for possibilities to have full expressions in God's plan and purpose concerning you.

In case you have lost your confidence in God, or about the future, or in the promises of God, stand up and renew it. God is not afraid of failures, he is only concerned about your faithlessness and hopelessness, when you renew your faith and your hope about the future, your future will be handled by God to submit to you.

4. UNCERTAINTY

When hope fades away, life will be filled with uncertainty, existence will become meaningless, and purpose will be filled with unclearity.

When you come into this situation in your life, you will discover that the promises of God even as strong as they are cannot give any meaning to your life because your life is already filled with fear, threats, worries, sorrow, and insecurity about what the future will become.

Child of God, never you come into a time in your life that you will allow hopelessness to cloud your future, and disconnect you from the promises of God's word.

God has a bright future for you, you need to believe it, you need to hold on to it by faith, and with strong conviction until the reality of that future is established in your life.

Hope empowers you to suppress the pains and afflictions of bad circumstances in your life, and to look beyond the effect of bad situations to hold unto better promises of God until your faith is being vindicated with answered prayers.

God is awakening the dead future of your life, God is reviving every hope that has faded away in your life, your faith that is dead is quickened to be alive from today, you need to hold unto God again, there is restoration of a better tomorrow in your life.

REVELATION OF BETTER FUTURE

Seeing into your future as a believer with your eyes of faith is an act of seeing and believing that the promises of God concerning you, and for your existence shall come to pass as a miracle in the nearest future without contradictions.

Seeing into your future as a child of God with your eyes of hope is the act of standing firm in the promises of God for your future with strong convictions that God is going to make dreams, aspirations, and vision to become favourable to you, no matter what the oppositions may seem to be.

If God says that you will be rich, believe it as your future for it must surely come to pass.If the promise of God for your life is that you cannot serve money, believe it because according to God's word, money is under obligation to obey your command.

If God says that prosperity and success will abide in your dwelling place, believe it for that is your future in Christ, even though you are not seeing it today, surely you shall see it is coming to pass tomorrow as your reality.

Beloved, the gap between your today and your future is luck and fate, if God steps into your life today, it means that the future that he promised you has come to unfold itself as your tomorrow miracle. The good news is that God has stepped into your life today according to his diving timing, that future you think that it is not possible will surely unfold itself in the activities of your life as a miracle from heaven.

When luck is released into your life, the vacuum created in your destiny by failures shall be filled up, when fate has been decided that activities of life in the affairs of man shall begin to work in your favour you will discover that that your future is not tomorrow as you think, rather your future is just a better today that is prepared to keep getting better day by day until you become what God made you to be.

Child of God, your hope is healed now, your hope is made alive again, luck and fate has come to play a role in your life, your poverty shall fade away, and financial blessings shall take its rightful place in your destiny.

CHAPTER 4

ABOVE ONLY

According to divine placement, and positioning where you have a place is on the top, and being in the top includes being in control of financial dominion and prosperity.

As a child of God you are not permitted to be in the tight corner of poverty, and be disadvantaged financially in your walk with God.

By the virtue of the covenant blessing you are saved to be blessed, you are redeemed to prosper, and you covenanted in the word of God to be a testimony of financial prosperity in all your life endeavours.

"And it shall come to pass, if thou shalt hearken diligently
Unto the voice of the Lord thy God, to observe and to do all
his commandments which I command thee this day, that the Lord
thy God will set thee on high above all nations of the earth.
Deuteronomy 28:1.

You are begotten by God to be set upon all the nations of the earth, which simply means that greatness, unequalled success, outstanding achievement, and financial dominion that leads to riches and wealth is your portion of blessing in Christ.

Child of God, God is taking you to the top, God has a place for you on the top, you are living a low financial position in life, and you are coming out from the plague of poverty to celebrate your financial liberty, and freedom in Jesus Christ.

"And the LORD shall make thee the head,
And not the tail, and thou shall be above only,
And thou shall not be beneath, if that thou shall hearken unto the
Commandment of the Lord thy God, which I command thee
This day, to observe and to do them
Deuteronomy 28:13

You are leaving the beneath places of life this moment, it is abomination according to redemption for you to be the tail in life.

Your destiny is living the place of a low life experience to be positioned in the financial future that is year portion in life.

Friend, let faith arise in your heart, and let the realities of faith raise your spirit man to believe that the word of God has the power to validate the promises of God in your life as a believers, irrespective of the kind of situation that you are facing right now that has enslaved you in poverty, and has silenced you to seat in the back corner of life.

RE ARRANGEMENT OF THE LADDER

Many people are being kept in the valley of financial frustration, how can you come out of the valley to climb up in life when there is no ladder to bring youup.

Many believers are being held captive in the dungeon of poverty, how can they come out of such pit to take their place in financial prosperity if God did not set up a ladder that can lead to their deliverance.

Many believers in this dispensation are being held bound in the pit of economic hardship in their business, finances, and life aspiration, how can this people come out from such pit to take their place in financial dominion when there is no ladder that can link them to their financial position in Christ.

Child of God, there shall be re-arrangement of the ladder in your life, God will give you a lift that will take you out of the valley of poverty to place you in the position of financial prosperity.

***"The LORD maketh poor, and maketh rich,
He bringeth low, and lifted up.
He raised up the poor out of the dust, and lifteth up the bigger from the Dungeon, to set them among princes, and to make them inherit the throne Of glory, for the pillars of the earth are the Lord's and he hath Set the world upon them.***

1Samuel 2:7-8

God is about to shake the pillars of the earth for your sake, and impossibilities shall become possible in your financial situations.

Heaven is bringing down a ladder to the saints of God, and this ladder shall serve has a link that will help you out of the pit of poverty to lead you to your financial placement in life.

WHAT IS A LADDER?

A ladder is what you can climb to leave a place where you are to the place where you want to be, and where you suppose to be.

A ladder is what gives you a link to leave a particular position that is not favourable, to take your place in that position that is favourable.

A ladder is what helps you out of frustration and limitations of life that you found yourself because of your background to link you to new height in life where you are well positioned in life to enjoy sudden change of status that has no respect to your background.

There shall be a re-arrangement of ladder in the body of Christ this end-time, the saints of God are about to enter into a new phase of life, and a new order of breakthrough experience that will take place as a supernatural occurrences of God in the financial matters of his children in the economyof nations in this dispensation.

"Blessed is the people that know the joyful sound;
They shall walk,
O LORD, in the light of thy countenance. For thou art the glory of their strength,
And in thy favour our horn shall be exalted.

Psalm 89:15, 17.

Today is the day of help for you, you shall surely encounter the help of God in the situation that has reduced you to nothing in poverty.Anywhere that poverty has subjected you to helplessness and it seems that is no link for you to come to the top, there shall be a re-arrangement of the ladder for you in that situation that will bring you out of poverty to place you in the position of financial liberty, that will be your testimony.

CHAPTER 5

RECOVERING THE STARS OF JACOB

According to redemption you are born to be a star in destiny, and by the blessing of redemption every star in the kingdom of God is ordained by God to hold a lamp of financial dominion, destiny business as a sign appointed to follow the redeemed of the Lord.

"And their seed shall be known among the gentiles,
And their offspring among the people;
All that see them shall acknowledge them, that they are the seed
Which the LORD hath blessed.

Isaiah 61:9.

Child of God, Jacob is a seed of Abraham, and by the virtue of the covenant you are ordained to be the seed of Abraham, and to be a star in Jacob. God met with Jacob and changed his name to Israel to become a nation that will beget the great people of God across the nations of the earth through the finished work of salvation.

Salvation came to confirm that you are ordained to be a star in life as a fulfillment of the prophecy that went forth before time concerning Jacob that through his descendants in the lineage of Abraham kings, rulers, noblemen, princess, and stars shall emerge in the nation of covenant people, and in the fold of the saints.

"How goodly are thy tents, O Jacob, and thy tabernacles,
O Israel as the valley are they spread forth,
As gardens by the river side, as the trees of high does which the LORD
Hath planted, and as cedar tree beside the waters,
And his king shall be higher than Agag, and his kingdom
Shall be exalted.

Numbers 24:5-7

The promise that God made to Jacob that stars will emerge out of his loins, simply means that men who will control financial greatness, financial dominion, royalty, riches and wealth in the global economy shall proceed from the house hold of God, and come out among the saints to raise their ruling horns in the global business among the nations of the earth.

"There shall come a star out of Jacob,
And a scepter shall rise out of Israel.
Out of Jacob shall come he that shall have dominion,
And shall destroy him that remaineth in the city.
Numbers 24:17b, 19

To be a star in Jacob simply means to have a ruling horn with ordination to become great in life, to raise your head as an achiever in life, and to have dominion over the economy of your nation in such a way that you are walking in the blessing out of season, and in season without the limitations of the life.

To be a star of Jacob his to be positioned in the covenant that God made with father Abraham that his descendants will not suffer poverty, or become victims of circumstances, or financial crisis in life because they are ordained with the baton and mantle of the covenant to walk in the realities of supernatural blessings.

"Neither shall thy name any more be called Abraham;
For a father of many nations have I made thee.
And I will make thee exceeding fruitful, and I will make nations of thee;
And kings shall come out of thee.
Genesis 17:5-6.

You are ordained a descendant of Abraham in the covenant to walk in the blessing, and one of the terms of the covenant is that you are not permitted to be poor, to suffer financial calamity, neither are you allowed to lack the evidence of financial abundance in your walk with God as believer.

Then anywhere your star has been stolen, caged, or being held captive in life, business and destiny that has made you to bow your head to poverty, and surrendered to low life, there shall be a release, a recovery, and a restoration taking place in your life.

To be a star simply means to have money as your servant, and to have upper hand over the negative effects of the economic situation under your control.

To be a star is to be a believer that is supernaturally positioned in the covenant of God to walk in the blessing that makes ordinary men rulers, kings, and men of dominion in the financial realm at all times.

By the grace of God, God is bringing you to this position where you will not be a victim of financial struggles that has made many believers to bow their heads in shame, mockery, and reproach, and compromise the Christian faith.

MONEY POWER IS OUR KINGDOM INHERITANCE

Money has the power to decide destinies, fate, events and outcome of situations.

Money has a great influence over the existence of mankind to the extent that the people that has it in abundance are men that has power, voice, and authority in the society, in nations and in the world today.

But the truth remains that money power is the inheritance of the saints in the kingdom of God.

Child of God, the kingdom of God is the kingdom of wealth, and riches, there is no poverty in the kingdom of God.

"I will speak of the glorious honour of thy majesty,
And of thy wondrous works.
They shall speak of the glory of thy kingdom,
And talk of thy power. Thy kingdom is an everlasting kingdom,
And thy dominion endureth throughout all generations.

Psalm 145:5, 11, 13

The kingdom of God is the kingdom that understands the language of royalty, and power which includes spiritual power, economic power, and money power. There is no kingdom that will have authority over the affairs of life, and be in control of life issues in the activities of nations without being in control of money power.

Money power is one of kingdom inheritance of the saints that the devil is contending with in this dispensation, but the good news is that battle has been won, the children of the kingdom shall rise again to control money power, economic power, and royalty globally in this dispensation in the activities of nations.

CONVERSION OF WEALTH AND RICHES

Conversion of wealth and riches is the work of God in the kingdom that initiate wealth transfer from the hand of the wicked, and the gentles to the hand of the covenant people of God.

Conversion of wealth and riches is a strange work and strange act of God that we cause the covenant people of God to inherit supernaturally the wealth and riches that the gentiles and the heathen labored for.

Child of God, anytime that the people of God started going through bad economy, economic hardship, financial crisis, and unending poverty in their nation, one of the covenant weapon that God uses to initiate their deliverance from poverty is conversion of wealth and riches that orders the gentiles nations and heathen to transfer their possessions, wealth, riches, and resources to the covenant people of God through a divine order.

For example, when God want to terminate economic and financial hardship of the Israelite God ordered the Egyptians to handover their resources, gold, and riches to the Israelites, and the word of God recorded that they left the land of Egypt with great favour, riches and wealth.

God is about to shake the pillars of the earth, the economy of nations shall be shaken, for the sake of the saints of God, and nations of the earth shall come under divine order to align their economy, market, and trade system to favour the people of God in this dispensation.

***"I will go before thee, and make the crooked places straight,
I will break in pieces the gates of brass and cut in asunder the bars of iron,
And I will give thee the treasures of darkness,
And hidden riches of secret places,
That thou mayest know that I, the lord which call thee by thy name,
Am the God of Israel.***

Isaiah 45:2-3

You are about to experience the miracle of conversion of wealth, financial fortune that will take place without struggles is about to take place in your life, when favour is involved, you will be empowered to reap where you did not sow, and harvest from places you did not do any labour.

CHANGE OF FINANCIAL POSITION

Your financial position is changing now, there shall be change of financial status for you.

The power that works for the saints is the power of God, and that power has the enabling grace that changes the financial position of man.You will become a man that will come out suddenly from the siege of financial hindrance to experience financial miracles in life.

The days of your sorrow and morning in poverty is over, a day is breaking forth in your business, finances, and personal economy.The fingers of God has appeared in the sky, and in the heavenlies to re-arrange the economic and financial position of the saints, and the body of Christ in the economy system of nations.

CHAPTER 6

COVENS THAT MAKES MEN RICH ARE NOT STRONGER THAN THE ANOINTING

There are some altars in the secret places of the kingdom of darkness, and occultic kingdom that are deceiving men to sacrifice their souls, and make human sacrifices in order to become wealthy and very rich.

Out of quest, for money many people have been led astray to patronize this devilish coven and money making charms in business with the intention that such gifts will make them to become rich and wealthy.

Child of God, the way that the ungodly prospers, is not the same that the believers are called by God to relate with prosperity of God's kingdom.

As a believer, you must understand that you cannot serve two masters at a time, you cannot believe in the gift of satan, and believe in the gift of God at the same time.

"Be sober, be vigilant, because your adversary the devil,
As a roaring lion, walketh about, seeking whom he may devour.
1Peter 5:8.

Don't allow the devil to deceive you with fake money, fake riches, and fake wealth that he will be parading this end-time to lead many people astray. There is a great compromise in the kingdom of God, many people who are once true believers in our Lord Jesus Christ, out of their lust for worldly riches, went to embrace evil covenant with occultic covens in order to become rich.

Many occultic covens and satanic altars that is leading souls astray with evil money, and occultic riches shall be disgraced by the waves of prosperity and anointing for godly riches and wealth that God is bringing down to confirm the manifold blessings of the saints in the church in this dispensation.

"The LORD is the portion of mine inheritance and my cup,
Thou maintainest my lot.
The lines are fallen unto me in pleasant places, yea, I have a goodly heritage.
Psalm 16:5-6

As a believer, you have financial inheritance in the kingdom of God in this dispensation, don't sell your soul to the devil because the covens that makes men rich in the kingdom of darkness are not stronger than the anointing. The anointing is stronger than the occultic satanic, and witchcraft covens that are making men rich as agents of darkness.

The anointing is stronger than the powers of darkness empowering men to excel with diabolic powers and charms in the business system.

The anointing will destroy every mockery of poverty in the lives of the saints in this dispensation to produce rich and wealthy men in the business system that will excel in life as godly men in the world system and give the believers a prosperity edge above the prosperity of the wicked and the ungodly in the market places.

FINANCIAL PERSECUTION OF THE WICKED

We are in the days when the kingdom of God shall be exalted above every other kingdom of this world. We are in the days when the wicked and evil doers who bowed to gods of baals for the sake of worldly and ungodly riches shall be persecuted in your life, you to taste a new breathe in financial prosperity.

The reason why Jesus Christ came was to destroy all the oppressions of the devil which includes the afflictions of poverty, lack and want.

"How God anointed Jesus Christ with Holy Ghost,
And with power, who went about doing good,
And healing all that were oppressed of the devil, for God was with him.
Acts 10:38

The afflictions of poverty is the same with the oppressions of sickness, and diseases because both of them came from the devil.

When you are held bound by the afflictions of poverty, somebody who is sick is even better than you.

But the truth remains that, Jesus Christ came with the anointing to break the yoke, afflictions, oppressions, and causes of poverty in your life to enable you to enjoy financial blessing as the goodness and kindness of God.

If you are walking in the pit of poverty, hopeless and helpless and nobody want to help you out, I want you to know that way out from the ancient poverty that is delaying your glorious destiny is your connection with the saving grace of

Jesus Christ, that is the foundation for your liberty from the curses of poverty that the devil hanged around your neck.

KEYS TO BREAK THE CURSES OF POVERTY IN YOUR LIFE

WITH CLEARITY OF DELIVERANCE TAKING PLACE IN YOUR LIFE

1. Desire to have raw encounter with the saving grace of Christ
2. Covert godly repentance, and turn away from sins
3. Embrace Christ as your Lord and personal Saviour
4. Believe in the hearing and doing the word of God
5. Trade with kingdom principles with obedience to God in your financial relationship with him.
6. Practice the covenant of liberal giving in the house of God
7. Obey the pastor and prophet that God gave to you to be giving over your life and over the works of your hands
8. Be a consecrated believer that practice godliness has a lifestyle
9. Hold tight the prophecies of your faith as a Christian for the hypocritics has no inheritance in Christ.
10. Be diligent in the works of your hands for God delights in the labour of the diligent.
11. Fervent in deliverance prayers that breaks every yoke of satan in the lines of the saints.
12. Serve God joyfully and faithfully for you cannot devote yourself to the service of God and be held bound by the plague of poverty.

CHAPTER 7

COMING OUT FROM SEVERE POVERTY

Severe poverty simply means a dangerous poverty that like a curse, and beyond it appears to be like it is going to last for a lifetime in the lives of those it is holding captive.

Severe poverty is a kind of poverty that has lasted so long in your life in such a way that people have mocked you and got tired, your relatives have reproached you and got tired.Your friends have left you, while your loved ones have despised you, and look down upon you because it appears like there is no hope, no help, and way out for you from your poverty experience.

All the brethren of the poor do hate him, how much more do his friends go far from him? he that pursueth with words, yet they are wanting to him.

Proverbs 19:7

When a man is held captive by severe poverty, that man will be like an accursed man among his people, and when a man stays in bad poverty for so long without any improvement on his situation, people will begin to count him among sinners.

Many people will begin to say who knows what he is doing against the Lord that made heaven to close their ears against his prayers.Who knows the kind of life that he is living in the secret that made God's goodness and mercies to forsake him?

Child of God, severe poverty is a devourer, a stigma, a reproach, a mockery, and enslavement that any believer must contend with, not to experience. Severe poverty is like a nemesis following someone with a remedy, it will be like a persecution, after some time it will attract afflictions to someone's life, and if nothing is done to stop it, it will settle as an oppression in the lives of a person.

Let my prayer come before thee, incline thine ear unto my cry. Mine eyes mourneth by reason of afflictions, Lord, I have called daily upon thee, I have stretched Out my hand unto thee.

Psalm 88:2, 9

Poverty is an oppression of the devil that must end in your life and severe poverty is an affliction of the wicked that must be terminated in your life by the reason of salvation power of Christ.

You are ordained to have victory over situations, but how can one be counted among the victorious among the saints when you have accepted defeat before poverty. How can you rejoice that you are an overcomer in Christ when there is no testimonies of victory over poverty that is taking place in your life as a Christian.

How do you become too spiritual, too holy, and too righteous as a believer yet you are suffering the defeat of poverty in your life as stigma that the devil placed upon your life to soil the works of the anointing upon your life.

Child of God, rise up from the place of your defeat because God is giving a second chance to walk into victory over poverty, God is restoring a new season, and a new timing for you to break away from every entanglement of poverty to enter into the physical realm of financial liberty, for that is the reason Jesus Christ died for you on the cross of Calvary.

For ye know the grace of our Lord Jesus Christ, that, though he was rick, yet for your sakes he became poor, that ye through his poverty might be rich.

2Corinthians 8:9

Jesus Christ took the position of poverty on the cross of Calvary for you to be rick, he came to break the yoke of hereditary and generational poverty in your life and in your family.

Christ came that you may more from grass to grace, rise from nobody to somebody, and come out of the value to take your place on the top.

Christ came to move you out o poverty to riches, from lack to abundance, from bad situations to better life, he came to make sure that your coming out of poverty is a reality.

Friend, it does not matter how bad, sorrowful, harmful and dangerous that your level of poverty seems to be right now, you are coming out of it mysterious by the hand of God.

KEYS TO BREAK AWAY FROM SEVERE POVERTY

1. DIVINE INSPIRATION: Divine inspiration is like an hammer that breaks the yoke of poverty without delay, when you become a man or woman that is inspired by God new ideas, creative spirit, and creative faith will be deposited upon your life to propel you by the spirit of God to know what is required of you to do to walk out of your ugly situations miraculous
2. STARTING A NEW BUSINESS: Child of God if you are being tormented by sever poverty and you have no job, start a new business, and if the business you are doing already is small you need to work towards expansion to connect yourself to supernatural flow of Divine multiplication, increase, streams of income, and profit enlargement.
3. BE DILIGENT: You need to wake up from your slumber and embrace diligence, there is no place on the top for a lazy man.

   One of the gift that salvation offers to you as a believer is ability to work hard, and trade with the talents that God bestowed upon you, and with the money that God committed into your hands until your financial growth is established.
4. FAITH TO TAKE RISK: Faith to take risk is the dimension that needs awakening among the saints in this dispensation. Faith to take risk is a dimension that cannot accept to faint even in contradictory situations until God makes a way where there is no way.

   There are miracles that use to follow the poor when they begin to walk in faith to change their situation, and these miracles are divine support, divine help, divine approval of God that causes men to favour you in your quest to make your life and situation better.

Coming out of severe poverty is a will of God, it is a prophetic declaration for you, but you need to act on it, by the virtues of the holyghost, you will see the plagues of poverty being subjected and disgraced in your life with an open victory and testimonies in the mighty name of Jesus Christ.

CHAPTER 8

BREAKING ANCIENT CURSES OF POVERTY

There are promises of God that cannot be a reality in your life even though they are your own, until the curses of poverty are broken drastically in your life from your ancient foundation to your family background.

The reason why many people are poor, even after they are saved with the saving grace of Jesus Christ is because there are powers that are opposing their financial blessings from their biological root.This powers have vowed that they can never walk in the realities of financial liberty throughout their lifetime.

Child of God, salvation came to save you from the bondage of sin, and to break the curses of poverty in your life, but when there are powers that are opposing your blessings of reality from seeing the light of the day, what you need to establish your victory in Christ in your finances is the deliverance power of God.

BE CONNECTED TO THE DELIVERANCE POWER OF GOD

Salvation is ordained to establish the promises of God for your life, but deliverance is ordained to destroy oppositions that is fighting against the manifestation of the promises of God in your life.

The deliverance power of God has the anointing and virtues that can break the curses of ancient poverty in your life, business, finances, and family as a Christian.

But upon Mount Zion shall be deliverance, and there shall be holiness; and the house of Jacob shall possess their possessions.
Obadiah 17

When the ancient curses are at work in your life, what you need to break it is the deliverance power of God, you need understand that deliverance is not about praying, it also involves personal intercession before the lord to move his hand into your affairs to do his strange works in your life.

Child of God, deliverance is not all about fasting and praying alone, it also has to do with application of the knowledge of God, biblical revelations, and paying attention to the mysteries of God's kingdom with a heart of disobedience to attract the hand of God to work in your affairs so as to clear every oppositions in your life physically and spiritually that is hindering his promises from coming to pass in your life.

Thy word is a lamp unto my feet, and a light unto my path. The entrance of thy word giveth light, it giveth understanding unto the simple.

Psalm 119:105, 130

Deliverance is to use the light of God's word to destroy oppositions to your blessings, and to establish the liberty of Christ in your life to walk in the realities of better things, and better promises according to the promise that Christ brought to you in salvation.

ANCIENT CURSES OF POVERTY MUST BE BROKEN IN YOUR LIFE

Ancient curses of poverty must be broken in your life, when that is done, money shall be your slave and not your enemy.

The reason why many believers who have met the requirements to walk in financial blessings are far away from it, is not because God has not released the blessing to them, but because there are ancient curses of poverty in their life from your foundation that is forcefully resisting and opposing the blessings from becoming a reality in their lives as believers.

If the foundations be destroyed, what can the righteous do?

Psalms 11:3

The foundations of family background and ancestral root is the reason why many believers are suffering in life, when there is an ancient curse of poverty in your family foundation one of the signs that will be following you is deprivation of financial blessings.

SIGNS TO SHOW THAT ANCIENT CURSES OF POVERTY IS AT WORK IN YOUR LIFE.

1. **UNENDING SUFFERING:** When the curses of ancient curses of poverty are at work in your life, one of the signs that use to follow it is unending

suffering. It is not the will of God for you to suffer throughout your lifetime as a believer, God ordained suffering to be a temporary thing with an end that will reveal His glory in your situation as a believer.

2. **EATING FROM HAND TO MOUTH:** Eating from hand to mouth is a curse that is following many people even in the house of God, when this curse is upon a man, that man can never have enough, abundance or sufficiency in his life. The plague of lack and want will be following him in his business, finances, even in his family. It is not the will of God for you to be a believer that is far from the realities of biblical promises that offered you sufficiency as one of your blessings in Christ.

3. **FRUITLESS LABOUR:** Fruitless labour is one of the negative signs that use to follow ancient curses of poverty, when there is a curse upon your finances, and business, you will discover that all your effort, dreams and aspirations in life will yield the desired fruit according to your expectations. When this curse is upon the works of your hands you will discover that profit is not answering to your handworks, and favour will be out of your reach. It is not the will of God for you as a believer to be labouring under a curse, for by the virtue of covenant that follow the redeemed of the lord, poverty is under obligation to fade away in your life, for prosperity to take its place in your labour as a believer.

4. **FRUITLESS PRAYERS:** When the curses of ancient poverty is at work in your life one of the signs that you will be experiencing in your Christian life is fruitless prayers. Fruitless prayer is prying for years without any sign of answered prayers reflecting in your situation, circumstances, or in your finances. Fruitless prayers is fasting and prayers, and waiting upon the lord for days, months, and years that does not bring the realities of divine visitations to your life in terms of changing things around you for you to experience better days, a better life, and a better future. It is not the will of God for you to be a prayer giant, a prayer warrior, and a prayer pillar without any sign of financial blessings in your life.

5. **CAPITAL LOSSES AND EMPTY POCKET:** When ancient poverty is working in your life as a curse, one of the experience that you will have regularly in your business is capital losses, folding up of businesses, and emptiness following you. This are the kinds of afflictions and oppressions of the devil that cannot allow a man to have money that belong to him, or with a reasonable amount of money as a business man. When this curse is upon your life, it will empty your bank account, destroy your capitals, and disconnect you from the flow of profits so as to close the sources of your livelihood on a regular basis. If you find yourself under this kind of experience, they shall be a deliverance for you, for it is not the will of God for you to be a man that have nothing, a man that is valueless in life, a man who is living a begging life.

6. **DWARF BUSINESS AND LITTLE PROGRESS:** If ancient poverty is working in your life as a curse of the experience you will be having in your life is dwarf business, and little progress.

   Dwarf business is a business that has refused to grow, a business that has refused to lead you to achievement, a business that is yielding little progress. When you find yourself under this situation, one of the bad occurrences that you will be going through is delayed blessings, crawling success, failure at the edge of breakthrough, business intentions and crisis. It is not the will of God for you as a believer to be under the siege of dwarf business, dwarf blessings, and little progress, this experience is fading away in your life today henceforth by the making of the most high God.

7. **ROAD BLOCKAGES:** When the road blockers are after your life physically and spiritually, one of the experiences you will be going through in your life and business is strong hindrances to favour, and severe attacks against every door that is opening for you to escape poverty.

   When you are held captive by road blockers, you will be going through unrealistic prosperity, that is prosperity that come your way, and was celebrated but could not see the light of the day, rather it turned to sorrow in your life and disappeared from being your open testimonies.

In the book of Isaiah chapter 48:15, the word of God says ***"I, even I, have spoken; yea, I have called him, I have brought him, and he shall make his way prosperous."***

God has ordained your ways to be prosperous, which means that your prosperity cannot be like a dream that fades away before the morning time. Many people are in the cage of road blockages. This is a curse that makes sure that breakthrough is not possible in your life, family and business. This is a kind of curse that makes sure that any way of escape that you discover to move yourself out of severe hardship is frustrated never to yield the desired results for you; this is the kind of curse that makes sure that opportunity for upliftment does not come your way.

In anyway you are labouring under a spoiled opportunity, God is mending your broken life, and your broken walls and the outcome of it is that opportunities shall run towards you to embrace you, and shall stand with you to lift you up as a living success.

8. **HELPLESS AND HELPLESS HELPERS:** When ancient poverty is working in your life as curse, one of the negative occurrences that you will be experiencing is helplessness, no matter what you do to access help in a hopeless situation, you will discover that help will be far away from you. Every attempt to connect yourself to right helpers will be frustrated by strange signals coming from places that is beyond your control. When you find yourself under this experience, you will discover that the people that will surround you are helpless helpers. These kinds of helpers are helpers that are living to help you in your situation, but they are not empowered with resources that they need to make your life better, or to grant you a relief in your situations.

Child of God, to find yourself in the midst of helpless helpers for a long time is a bad occurrence among such a people, you will be vulnerable to bad situations for years without any change taking place in your life until the lord sends you to the right place where your potential helpers of destiny are waiting for you.

WHO CURSED YOU?

Curses are not the inheritance of the children of God, rather blessings are your portion in Christianity.

It does not matter how the curse came upon your life, the good news is that they must be broken. In case, it is God that cursed you, by the sure mercies of David, the most high God shall withdraw his anger and hand of chastisement upon your life for you to experience a change of story in your financial life.

For a small moment have I forsaken thee, but with great mercies will I gather thee.
In a little wrath I hid my face from thee for a moment, but with everlasting kindness will I have mercy on thee, saith the Lord thy Redeemer.

Isaiah 54:7-8

If it is God that cursed you, by the release of his everlasting covenant, the curse is broken in your life, if it is an angel of God that laid the curse upon your life because of your sins towards God, and the works of God, from today the curse is broken in your life, and upon the works of your hands.

Friend, if the curse came into circulation upon your life and begins to torment you in different aspect of your life through the foundation of your father's house, from today henceforth, the embargo is lifted, and the siege is broken for you to be a reflection of financial blessings in your Christian life.

Everything you lost in life as a result of afflictions of ancient poverty shall be restored and recovered back to you in a million fold.

If the curse came to your life as the result of the oppressions of the wicked upon your life, business, and finances there shall be a vindication in your favour, for everything they did to humiliate you with poverty shall backfire, and go back to live as an everlasting affliction upon your enemies, and upon their generation for that is the verdict of God's word.

For thus saith the Lord of hosts, after the glory that he sent me unto the nations which spoiled you; for he that touched youtoucheth the apple of his eyes.
For behold, I will shake mine hand upon them, and they shall be a spoil to their servants, and ye shall know that the Lord of hosts hath sent me.

Zechariah 2:8-9

God shall render recompense to those that persecuted your blessings, he shall render judgement to those that stand as oppositions to the fulfilment of biblical promises of God upon your life as a believer. For you shall rise, but they shall collapse, your head shall be lifted up, but they shall bow their head in shame before your presence.

KEYS TO BREAK THE CURSES OF ANCIENT POVERTY IN YOUR LIFE IN A MOMENT

1. **PRAYER OF MERCY:** Prayer of mercy is not made just for those who are pleading for forgiveness of sins from God, it is also prayer allowed to be prayed for believers who want God to step into their hopeless and helpless situations with his loving kindness, compassion, and pity.

   In the book of Hebrew chapter 4:16 the word of God declares, "Let us therefore come boldly unto the throne of grace, that we may obtain mercy, and find grace to help in the time of need.

   There is a virtue, grace and anointing that flows in the prayer of mercy ordain to break ancient curses, including the curses of poverty. When the power that flows in the prayer of mercy is provoked to come down, one of the remarkable signs that will take place in your life is that the veil of poverty shall be folded up in your life suddenly like a garment.

2. **HOLINESS:** Holiness is the key that you need to retain the work of deliverance in your life so as to enjoy and endless blessings of God. When you begin to live a holy life according to Obadiah 17, there shall be a release of your portion, inheritance and possessions in Christ as a believer.

3. **SALVATION:** Salvation is the key that you need to break the ancient curses of poverty in your life, in case you have not made Christ your personal Lord, and saviour you need to proclaim him as your saviour. Above that, you need to walk in the realities of genuine salvation with a decision to live a dedicated life to the will of God, a life that is pleasing in the sight of God in all your ways.

4. **PREPENTANCE FROM REBELLION:** Repentance from rebellion is the key you need to break the ancient curses of poverty in your life. If you are a child of God that is rebelling against God, and against the word of God. You need to turn away from your evil ways to embrace obedience to the word of God as a lifestyle, and as a daily habit, for when your obedience is tested and trusted in the sight of God, there shall be reward in your life.

5. **KINGDOM SERVICE:** In the book of Mathew 6:33 the word of God says ***"But seek ye first the kingdom of God, and his righteousness, and all these things shall be added unto you."***

   Kingdom service that is engaged with passion and zeal to the prosperity of the house of God is the key that you need to break the ancient curses of poverty in your life, business and finances. If poverty is encroaching into your life, engage yourself in the service of God's kingdom without compromise, and you will discover that ancient poverty shall collapse in your life like a broken wall, and a cracked fence.

6. **RADICAL FINANCIAL SACRIFICES:** Radical financial sacrifice is the key that breaks the ancient curses of poverty in a moment without delay. Radical financial sacrifice simply means giving an amount of money to God that cost you a lot, an amount of money that seems to be the whole money that you have in life.

   Radical financial sacrifice simply means giving to God the amount of money that is beyond your capacity to remove out of your business, or investment with a faith in your heart, that it will return back with a financial promotion that answers to you and your access to riches and wealth without struggles.

   If poverty is tormenting your finances, business, and the works of your hands, take a financial sacrifice and release it to God at the altar of God in the sanctuary and you see the bad effects of sever poverty disappear in your life, for a new hope of prosperity to start appearing in your life pursuit.

   Radical financial sacrifice simply mean to give to God with a large heart, a times it is the act of giving to God everything you have in life, in your bank account, or everything you have left with you after going through a sever hardship and financial crisis.

Gather my saints together unto me; those that make a covenant with me by sacrifices.

Psalms 50:5

Financial sacrifice is the key to provoke the covenant of prosperity in the kingdom of God, and when the covenant is set at work in your life, there is no curse of poverty that can stand against you no matter how severe it may appear to be in operation.

7. **A NEW DIMENSION OF TITHING:** Biblical requirement for tithe payers is ten percent, but when a man wants to provoke the acts of God in his circumstances, such a man is required to engage the act of faith to command the appearance of the supernatural and the miraculous to get his expectation established as a reality. A new dimension of tithing simply means an act of faith that provokes you voluntarily to engage yourself in giving to God more than ten percent of your earning so as to walk in uncommon financial miracles, and financial favours.

   When you come into this realm, and into the fold of the believers that walks with God in this dimension, there is no force of hell that can keep you under the siege of poverty, neither can they stop your prosperity from happening.

8. **COVENANT PARTNERSHIP:** Covenant partnership is the key to break the ancient curses of poverty, covenant partnership is the act of dedicating your money, resources, business, to do the work of God in the house of God, and under pastoral ministry, and instructions.

   Covenant partnership is to commit your finances to service the needs of God's house as service to God, and the sanctuary and among the saints.

And God is able to make all grace abound toward you, that yea, always having all sufficiency in all things, may abound to every good work.

2Corinthians 9:8

Covenant partnership is a financial service in the house of God that can make money to flow to you from all nations in different currencies no longer out of your labour, but out of favour. When you begin to render financial services to God in the house of God, you have made yourself a partner with God, and when you step into that position, there is a realm of grace that will open into you to make sure that you are not sloughing to make money, rather money will begin to run and fly towards you in submission to covenant of wealth in the kingdom of God.

9. **DIVINE ALIGNMENT TO THE MINISTRY OF THE PROPHETS:** Divine alignment to the ministry of the prophets is the key to break the ancient curses of poverty in your life, business, and finances. Divine alignment to the ministry of the prophets simply mean to come under the leadership, teaching, guidance, instructions and ministry of a prophet that God brought to your path as a covering over your life, finances, business, and your connection of grace into the realms of success and prosperity for believers in the kingdom of God.

Believe in the Lord your God, so shall ye be established, believe his prophets so shall ye prosper.

2Chronicles 20:20b

There is anointing for prosperity and success that God deposited in the ministry of the prophets ordained to break every curse of ancient poverty in your life, and to eliminate their negative effects, and stigma in your life.

When you align yourself to be an obedient follower and disciple to the ministry of your God ordained prophets, one of the signs that will start following you, your business, and the works of your hands is divine empowerment.

Divine empowerment is the release of approval, recommendation, and unlimited grace in your direction that orders the favour that are not looking for you to start running towards you to build up your destiny and your vision in life. When divine empowerment is at work in your life as a grace and as a sign ordained to follow you with the favour and opportunities that you are no looking for will be looking for you to bless you.When this has become your experience, there is no way that the plague of poverty will not cease to raise its ugly hand in your life.

10. **DELIGHT IN THE PROSPERITY OF MEN OF GOD:** To delight in the prosperity of men of God is the key to break the ancient curses of poverty upon your life. When you see a servant of God prospering, do not envy him or mock the blessings of God upon his/her life for such habit or character can bring the curse of the Lord upon your life.

    As a believer, when you see a servant of God in need, or suffering from poverty, instead to mock him, and laugh at him, be a stone of help around him in that period of his life, such character, and ministration of help can cause the yoke of poverty to be broken in your life like a dream of the night.

    Let them shout for joy, and be glad, that favour my righteous cause, yea, let them say continually, let the Lord be magnified, which hath pleasure in the prosperity of his servants.

    Psalms 35:27

    When you choose to stand as a helping hand to a man of God to fulfil his calling, and succeed in the ministry, you have positioned yourself to be a man that will be under an open heaven in all your life aspirations, and it is God that opens the heavens upon your life, business, and finances, no fire of hell can stop you from commanding prosperity.

CHAPTER 9
MAKING MONEY IS A GRACE

Money answereth all things that pertains to the need of man, but the truth s that nobody can make money and gather it in abundance if the grace of God is not with him.

Making money whatever you do in life s by the grace of God, grace is what makes the difference between those that are making money in life and those that are struggling in life.

WHAT IS GRACE

Grace is the gift of God that empowers you to become what you cannot be by your power, and enables you to do what you cannot do by your strength, and allows you to have access to possessions and privilege that is not common among men.

Grace is the virtue of God that empowers men, ordinary men, to have the understanding and initiative to do something that can attract profits, and order money to flow to their direction until prosperity becomes possible, and riches becomes a reality.

"Let thy hand be the man of thy right hand,
Upon the son of man whom thou madest strong for thyself
Turn us again, O LORD God of hosts, cause thy face to shine,
And we shall be saved.

Psalms 80:17, 19

Making money is a grace, the difference between the poor and the rich is not hardwork, rather it is grace of God. The difference between the elite and common people is grace, is not hardwork.When grace is not available even the opportunity to do things that can generate money that people can refer to as hardwork will be deprived.

MAKING PROFIT IS DIVINE

Making money is a grace, and making profit is divine, until you come into the realm where the flow of profit has accepted your person, you cannot be a man that can be referred to as a prosperous man, or as a rich man. Making profit is divine because God is the author of multiplication increase, and expansion, making profit is the divine because God is the initiator of business, success, and prosperity with the intention to enhance the survival of man, and to confirm the blessings of covenant people.

"Thus saith the LORD, thy redeemer, the HOLY
One of Israel, I am the Lord thy God
Which teacheth thee to profit, which leadeth thee by the way
That thou shouldest go.

Isaiah 48:17

God is bringing you to a position where you will have the opportunity to make money, God is bringing you unto a place where profits will be flowing to you like the rushing waves of mighty oceans in that your business, and in that vision, they shall be a new revolution in the works of your hands.

THERE IS A DELIVERANCE IN YOUR FIELD OF WORK

There is a deliverance in your field of work, and this deliverance is divine initiative to destroy anti-profit devourers that is frustrating you from making money and from recording growth in your endevours.

The deliverance is divine because it is going to bridge between you and the rich, between you and the wealthy.In such a way that you become a man that will join the company of the rich, and the wealthy as a man whom the grace of God has empowered to make money, and to generate profit in restricted ways.

Child of God, by the virtue of this deliverance, that same business, job and visions that is not working for you, and it is not generating big money, and has no opportunity for you to be make big profits in it, shall turn around to bless you miraculously, because the following deliverance will surely take place in your life.

1. **YOKES STRUGGLES ARE BROKEN:** When grace is involved in your life, it will break the yokes of struggles, and make you a man that will be prosperous in life.

   The reason why may people are struggling to make money is because grace is withheld, when grace is at work, it will terminate your struggles, and make life to treat you with kindness in such a way that the work of your will attract prosperity and success in unlimited fold such that can make you rich, and meet your needs according to your desires.

Your struggles in life, and business is ending today because grace has come to play a role in your quest to make money, and to generate profit in your endeavours.

2. **YOKE OF HARDLUCK AND BADLUCK ARE BROKEN:** The opposite of hardluck is goodluck, luck has great role to play in the success of man, luck is the supernatural in nature, and in occurrence, it is factor that is ordained by God to reward the labour of a man, and to live the labour of another man unrewarded.

   Atimes, the difference between a man that is prospering in life, and the man that is not prospering is luck even though both of them may be in the same business, luck is what is ordained to determine the blessing that will rest upon their hardwork, and their business pursuit.

"I returned, and saw under the sun, that the race is not to the swift,
Nor the battle to the strong, neither yet bread to the wise,
Nor yet riches to men of understanding,
Nor yet favour to men of skill, but time
And chance happeneth to them all.
Ecclesiastes 9:11

If hardluck is following you, what you need is for luck to smile in you and you will discover that things will turn around for good for you, in the same place that life has worked against you in the past.

There is a change in the realm of occurences of luck for you, and for the works of your hands, from today luck will start working yin your faovur, and fate will begin to treat you with kindness, you shall surely experience this deliverance in the name of Jesus Christ.

3. **THE YOKE OF MISFORTUNE ARE BROKEN:** The opposite of misfortune is fortune, the yokes of misfortune are broken in your life now, and the siege of crises, calamities, sorrow, losses, and dissapointment that is following your endeavours shall cease to reflect and appear in your life.

   Because God is closing their windows in the works of your hand, this shall surely be your experience in the mighty name of Jesus Christ.

There is a deliverance initiated by God to envelope the field your work to enhance your labour with supernatural breakthrough in a million fold dimension, I see you recovering all that you have lost in that business, and in that investment sooner than you think by the help of God, and by the work of grace.

MAKING MONEY IS DIVINE ENDOWMENT UPON THE BELIEVERS

Making money is grace ordained to by God to function has divine endowment upon the believer, there is a new release of grace upon your life, this grace is given to the saints of God in this dispensation to command money, to control money, and to make money until the promise of prosperity, riches and wealth becomes a reality in the church of Jesus Christ this in this end-time.

1. **YOU ARE REDEEMED TO EXCEL IN LIFE:** By the virtue of redemption, it is your birthright in Christ to excel in life in whatever you lay your hands to do as your work.

   Child of God, excelling in life simply means to walk in progressive growth and achievement in all your endeavours as a sign that prosperity is certain in your life as a covenant child of God. If you are not excelling before in the works of your life, things will charge in your direction, grace is activated in the spirit realm to push you forward in the pursuit of your well-being among men.

2. **YOU ARE SAVED TO SUCCEED IN LIFE:** By the virtue of salvation, to achieve success is your birthright in Christ, you cannot be going backward when others are succeeding, because God has ordained with grace as a divine endowment to enhance your success to take a lead among your peers in this dispensation.

   If you are far away from success as of today, there shall be repositioning in your life, and in the works of your hands, your next attempt to succeed in life will hit your desired targets in the name of Jesus Christ.

3. **YOU ARE DESTINED TO PROSPER:** You are destined to prosper in life, infact, prosperity is your birthright in the predestination plan of God.

   The purpose of God for your life is for you to walk in unrestricted prosperity, as a fulfilled of already detained destiny that belong to you in Christ.

   In the book of Romans Chapter 8:17 the word of God declares *"And if the children, then heirs, of God, and joint heirs with Christ, if so be that we suffer with him, that we may be also glorified together".*

   We are the heirs of God through the saving grace of Jesus Christ, prosperity is our birthright as children of the most High God, and for this reason, destiny must smile at you with unlimited prosperity. Infact, according to your birthright in Christ, it is not your destiny to become poor, or to be in poverty as an experience.

4. **YOUR ARE JUSTIFIED TO WALK IN THE BLESSING:** By the virtue of the justification of the spirit, there is no tongue, power, ruler, or kingdom on earth that has the authority to condemn your blessings, or disqualify you from relieving financial blessings.

   Child of God, you are justified by Christ with efficacy of the blood of the blood of the lamb to walk in the blessing, which means that even the accuser of the brethren, principalities, and powers, rulers of darkness in high places has no authority to withhold the flow of the blessing upon your life, or in your direction

   "For whom he did foreknow, he also did predestinate to be confirmed
   To the image of his son, that he might be the first born
   Among many brethren
   Moreover, whom he did predestinate, then he also called, and whom he called, then he also justified, and whom he justified, Them he also glorified.

   Romans 8:29-30.

Justification of the spirit, is the act of Christ that qualifies you to enjoy the blessings that you are not qualified but the work of grace came to qualify you to enjoy, and to empower you to become it.

The work of justification is the work of grace that silences the accusation of the brethren over the works of your hands to enable you to walk in the realities of financial blessings.

When the ministration of justification is at work in your life every condemnation that is restoring upon your life is restricted from prosperity, success, and financial blessings will be terminated and the outcome of it is that you will enjoy the flow of God's blessings as the work of grace, not by your personal merit.

"Wherefore in all things it be it behooved him
to be made like unto
His brethren, that he might be a merciful and faithful high priest in things pertaining to God, to make reconciliation for the sins of the people.
Hebrews 2:17.

Justification has prevailed in your case, and the veil of condemnation is folded upon the works of your hands, and upon your endeavours, there is a new beginning taking shape in your destiny, because grace has come to speak upon your life, that grace has spoken in your favour, and it has prevailed.

GET READY TO WALK IN THE PATH OF THE RCH AND THE WEALTHY

There is a path where the rich, and the wealthy are walking upon , for you to join the fold of the prosperous in the solitary in this dispensation you need to trace your way back, to reposition yourself to pursue life endeavours with clearity of purpose.

Child of God, to become rich and wealthy is God's promises for your life and grace has come to make it a reality, but you must understand that success in life at times does not answer to wishes, it answers to doing the right thing that is required to attract desirable success.

Making money is a grace, making money is your reality, but above all, making money is a work, you need to have a job to make money, you need to have a service point as a source of livelihood for you to generate income.

You need to be a problem solver for you to generate income, you need to have a skill and improve your skills in your endeavours.

You need to develop the gifts of God upon your life as divine activities, divine empowerment, divine deposit, and divine opportunity that God bestowed upon you a grace to attract money to flow to you and to reposition you in the ladder of prosperity.

You need to explore new opportunities for growth, and build upon the former achievement and exploit to create a room for God to bring large opportunity for breakthrough into your life, your business, and upon your establishment.

When you begin to act upon this things with faith, and with understanding, you will be enlisted by God among those that will walk in the path of the rich, and the wealth in your time. But above all, remember that walking in the path of the rich, and the wealth requires you to turn yourself into a new man by doing the following things.

1. **GET A NEW DREAM AND A NEW VISION:** It is time for you to dream again, it is time for you see visions again, for it is time for new dreams and new visions to strive, and lead to success is ripe in the dispensation grace, and your own dreams and visions must be among them.

2. **BE A WISE PLANNER AND A GOAL SETTER**: Wise planner are men with understanding of time, season, these are men who know how to set a goal, and achieve a goal.

   Wise planners are men who knows how to prepare for opportunities that are not yet ripe, and by the virtue of their preparation, if opportunity did not come their way, they will create one for themselves by God's grace at work upon their life.

   Child of God, stop waiting for tomorrow in uncertainty, rise up and prepare for your future aspiration, and it will be a surprise to you how this tomorrow will run after you with positivity.

3. **BE A CREATIVE THINKER AND SUCCESS INITIATOR:** You need to be a creative thinker for prosperity to smile at you, creative thinkers are men who knows how to put their future imaginations into a clear picture, and

create something in unique way to attract success that is not possible in their time.

Beloveth, you need to be a success initiator, if success refuse to come your way, initiate it by yourself by creating rooms. For wide improvement to keep taking place in your job, and in your business, when you do this properly, it is just a matter of time stubborn success that has rebelled against your personality for years shall bow at your feet.

4. **BE FOCUSED, BE PERSISTENCE, BE COURAGEOUS IN FACING RISK:** Be focus in life, do not allow distraction of life to remove you from the point of faith in the pursuit of your life endeavor. Be persistence in the midst of challenges, trials, and opposing circumstances in the line of your visions, it is just a matter of time, if you refuse to give up life will be kind to you to grant you your everlasting expectations.

   Child of God, be courageous in facing risks for the path of the great, the rich, and the wealth are filled with risky, only men of great courage can walk in it that path and overcome it. Only men with courage can see great pressures, and withstand, when you begin to experience certain things in the path of your success, stand firm in faith, and gird your loins in the faithfulness of God that cannot fail, and hold unto God's promises until your success is established as a living testimony.

   Beloveth, you are coming under the cloud of the blessed among the saints, the blessing of the cloud is coming upon you as covering over your success. You are coming under the cloud of the blessed in the body of Christ, the blessing of the dew is coming upon the works of your hands as covering over your prosperity.

   You are coming under the cloud of the blessed among the sons of God this end-time, the blessings of the heavens is resting upon your head as a seal of security upon your financial blessings says by the Holy Ghost, and nothing can stop it from becoming an existing reality.

CHAPTER 10

THE LIVING WORD IS YOUR SUFFICIENCY

The word is your sufficiency, there is no virtue, power and might that is able to build you up that is not flowing in the word of God.

The word of God is ordained with riches, wealth, and unsearchable treasures and precious things of God that can make a nobody to become somebody, and make a man who is rejected and cursed never to see any good thing in life to be a man who is dangerously blessed by God.

The word of god is ordained to make have all sufficiency, all abundance, and pleasant things that can lead to material blessing in life.

What is sufficiency? The word sufficiency simply means to have enough, more than enough, it means to have access to abundance, and to have whatever you need in excess.

Child of God, the word of God brought sufficient life to you to make you a man that will have eternal life in immeasurable ways, and to be a man that will have the manifold blessings and riches of God that positions you for material blessings in such that you will become a man that lacks nothing in faith and lacks nothing in reality.

My son, keep my words, and lay up my commandments with thee. Keep my commandments, and live, and my law as the apple of thine eye. Bind them upon thy fingers, write them upon the table of thine heart.

Proverbs 7:1-3

There are unsearchable riches of God that flows in the word of God ordained with the virtue of the spirits to break the yokes of poverty in your life, to connect you to the realities of material and financial blessings as your inheritance in Christ Jesus.

When thou encounter the unsearchable riches of God, in the word of God, you will become a man that walks miraculously in riches and wealth.

When you encounter the unsearchable riches of God, you will become a believer that walks in the realities of sufficiency and abundance in your business, finances, and material possessions. The unsearchable riches of God is ordained by God to give you inheritance as a believer in Christ, and this inheritance includes change of life, change of position, change of statusthat come as blessings of prosperity to abide with you.

The law of the Lord are perfect, converting the soul; the testimony

of the Lord is sure, making wise the simple.

The statutes of the Lord are right, rejoicing the heart; the

Commandment of the Lord is pure, enlightening the eyes.

Psalms 19:7-8

When you connect yourself to the word of God as your sufficiency, God will connect you to the unsearchable riches that flows in his word ordained to connect you to the foundation of material wealth in the kingdom of God, and these unsearchable riches of God's word are as follows:

1. INHERITANCE

There is an inheritance for you in the word of God as a child of God you have inheritance in the word of God, and your inheritance in the word of God includes financial blessings, financial prosperity and material possessions.

"According as his divine power hath given unto us all things that pertain unto life and godliness, through the knowledge of him that hath called us to glory and virtue"

2 Peter 1:3

The book of 2Peter 1:3 says that God has given to you all things that pertain to life and godliness, which means that your welfare, survival, future are secured in the word of God. God did it by handing over inheritance to you in the word of God.

When you begin to walk in this understanding deliverance from struggles, frustrations, sorrow will begin to happen in your life and finances.you will be able to trust God in the moment of hardship and suffering to know that he is your source, and it is from him that your liberation from financial hardship is going to become a reality, not from the economy of your nation, and not from the economy of this world.

Many believers who are messed financially in this dispensation shall bounce again in business to experience a better life because God is about to reveal his everlasting written wills as a documents that contains the inheritance of the saints in a distributed manner.

Child of God, there is an inheritance for you in the word of God that qualifies you to come to royalty, and live as a king in prosperity to rejoice in the wealth and riches that comes from god, and that is the chapter of your life that God is opening today henceforth, and you shall surely walk in it.

2. SURE PROMISES OF GOD

The sure promises of God contains the infallible promises of God for your life, and one of the promises of God for you is that you are adopted in the kingdom of God with a son-ship right after the order of Christ to enjoy the manifold blessings of God that forbids poverty, curses, low life, financial crisis to stick to your life or to your destiny.

For whom he did foreknow, he also did predestinate
to be conformedto the image of his son, that
he might be the firstborn among many brethren.
Romans 8:29

The word of God is a sure promise of God for you as a believer, when you begin to believe it, act on it, persist in obeying it by faith you will discover that impossibilities, limitations, and hindrances shall bow in your Christian, spiritual, financial life to give you an edge over failure, and make you a believer whose prosperity will become a delightful thing before God, and among the brethren.

3. MERCY AND TRUTH

One of the unsearchable treasures and riches of God that flows as a yoke breaking virtue in the word of God is mercy and truth, mercy and truth is ordained in the word of God connect you to God's everlasting kindness and goodness.

Mercy simply means compassion that shows to the needy, and a forgiveness that he reveals to people who are in need even in a moment that they don't deserve his attention, care, support.While truth is the revelation of God's ways, God's likeness, God's nature, and God's life that is being revealed to you as a child of God to connect you to the blessings of God's kingdom.

My son, forget not my law; but let thine heart keep my commandments.
For length of days, and long life, and peace, shall they add to thee.
Let not mercy and truth forsake thee, bind them about thy neck,

write them upon the table of thine heart.
So shall thou find favour and good understanding in the
sight of God and man.

Proverb 3:1-4

When you find the mercies of God, you shall walk in the unlimited kindness and goodness of God reveals God's generosity, liberality, supernatural provisions and supplies that fashions a believer that suffer hardship, lack, and want in the work of your hands.When that becomes your daily experience, it means that you are already at the centre of financial elevations that makes a man prosperous in life.

When you encounter the truth of God's word, light will begin to shine in your path, your darkness will disappear suddenly, and your better days shall appear suddenly to lunch you into the realm of believers who are walking in realities of better life in Christ.

When truth of God's word fills your heart, you will begin to walk in the fear of God, and any man that fears God according to the book of **Psalms 112:1-3** is not a man that cannot walk in the realities of financial prosperity and material wealth.

As you return back to God with your whole heart in truth and in spirit you will encounter the mercy and truth in God's word that will give you access to virtues ordained to break the yoke of financial frustrations and enslavement in the kingdom of God.

4. FAVOUR

Favour simply means what God can do that man cannot do, that God has done for his people, and he is still doing it for his people, in every generation and in every dispensation, favour is the supernatural works of God that reveals the possibilities of God to the helplessness of man in impossible situations.

Favour is the miraculous visitations of God in the limitations of his people that give them an edge over bad situations, ugly circumstances, and helpless life.

The Lord is righteousness in all his ways, and holy in all his works.
The Lord is nigh unto all them that call upon him, to all that call
upon him in truth. He will fulfil the desire of them that fear him,
he also will hear their cry, and will save them.

Isaiah 45:17-19

Favour is one of the unsearchable riches of God that flows in the word ordained to bring you into unlimited failure, good luck, and sudden prosperity in all your endeavours as a believer.

When the smells of favour is at work upon your life, doors will open in their own accord for you, your stories shall be filled with unusual positive experiences even at a time when others are going through severe tough times.

The word of God came to favour you, and through favour a believer is ordained to walk in the sufficiency of Christ that flows in the kingdom of God. Through favour the yoke of failure and object poverty will be broken in your life, and let me inform you that favour contains a yoke breaking power of God that can disgrace poverty, economic hardship, and cancel frustrations in the life of a believer anytime, and in any day.

May I prophecy to you, that the time for you to walk in financial favours has come, the time for you to walk in the sufficiency of God's word has come, and get ready because yokes are about to be broken in your life and they are falling apart in your life from today henceforth.

5. OPEN DOORS AND OPEN HEAVENS

Open doors is your portion in the word of God, and that is unsearchable riches of God that flows in the word of God to bless your life, open heaven is a precious thing in the kingdom of God ordained to open the ways of man, the aspiration of man, the visions of man, and the pursuit of man to meet with appointed help, helpers that makes the labour of man profitable on earth.

Child of God, there is an open door and open heaven for you in the word of God, when your doors are open, fortune will locate you without struggles, and when your heavens are open, your labour will begin to yield profitable fruits supernaturally in unusual manner.

I know thy works; behold, I have set before thee an open door, and no man can shut it, for thou hast a little strength, and hast kept my word, and hast not denied my name.

Revelation 3:8

When you connect yourself to walk in obedience to God's word you have connected yourself to open doors, and open heaves. It does not matter where you find yourself right, the gap between your poverty and your riches may be away from each other in accordance, but the hand of God shall bridge that gap in your affairs to make a miracle that supposed to take you many years to happen, to become a miracle that will happen in your life without struggle, delay, and oppositions.

6. DOMINION

Dominion simply means authority, power, and control given to you by God to have life working for you the way God ordained to be in your life, and the way you want it within the content of the provisions that God made available for you in the promises of his word.

> ***"For I know the thoughts that I think toward you, saith the Lord, thought of peace, and not of evil, to give you an expected end".***
> ***Jeremiah 29:11***

Dominion is the thought of God towards you, God want you to have dominion in life, God want life to be favourable to you, God want situations and circumstances to be under your control as a believer.

And for you to be a believer who is in control of situations, a man who has authority over circumstances, and a man who has power over the occurrences of events of life around him, you must be a man that walk in financial dominion.

Financial dominion is your birthright in Christ, because without financial dominion how can you walk in royalty, kingship, and priesthood in the kingdom of God as a believer.

From today, the yoke of financial enslavement, poverty imprisonment, and begging life is broken in your life, you are taking a position of a blessed man in the kingdom of God for that is your portion in the word of God.

7. BREAKTHROUGH POWER, MIRACLES, SIGNS AND WONDERS

There is a breakthrough power that is flowing in the word of God. You cannot be a believer and be held captive by the siege of closed door, blockages, and hindrances. There are miracles flowing in the word of God, you cannot be a child of God and live a life that is void of financial miracles.

There are signs and wonders flowing in the word of God, you cannot be a child of God and be void of prosperity and success following you as a sign that God is with you as the God who blesses, as the God who consecrate the blessed to become a blessing.

In the book of Isaiah 8:18 the word of God says "Behold, I and the children whom the Lord hath given to me are for signs and wonders."

If you are not walking in financial miracles before now, that dimension of encounter is open for you to be part of your life experience in all your endeavours from today.

From henceforth, you shall encounter breakthrough power of God, and what will be the outcome of it is your change of level and change of style.

CHAPTER 11

POWER OF THE COVENANT

The covenant is effectual in destroying the siege of darkness, the curses of Satan, and the authority of the gentiles upon the people of God in moments of trials, hardship, and suffering in a nation.

The covenant is a weapon of warfare in the kingdom of God that has the speaking power and voice to silence the manifold works of darkness, and the wicked in the affairs of covenant people of God.

The covenant in the kingdom of God simply means the promises of God for his people that God bound him to it with an oath, and with the integrity of his name to confirm it in the lives of his saints at all times, and in every circumstances and situations.

For who in the heavens can be compare unto the Lord? Who among the sons of the mighty can be likened unto the Lord? O Lord God of hosts, who is a strong Lord like unto thee? Or to thy faithfulness round about thee.

Psalms 89:6, 8

God is a covenant keeping God among hiss people, but he shall appear as God confirming and enforcing God to the saints of God in this generation.

Child of God, the covenant in the kingdom of God is superior to natural circumstances; It is higher and stronger than the operations of satan and kingdom of darkness in the affairs of men.At the rising of the covenant to speak greatness shall submit itself to the will of God concerning the people of God.

When the ark of the covenant appeared in the land of Egypt to speak for the deliverance, liberation, prosperity of the children of Israel, every protocols, and decree of kings were suspended, and the outcome of it is as that there was short of the miraculous and the supernatural in the camp of the Israelites.

May I prophecy to the cloud of this generation and the atmosphere of this dispensation that the ark of the covenant is coming down again from heaven to confirm the faithfulness of God to hiss promises for the saints in this generation, and by the reason of this strange works of God, ancient doors shall be opened, invisible barriers shall be broken, and the God of ancient economic captivity shall be broken in the camps of God's people in the national affairs of nations.

My covenant will I not break, nor alter the things that is gone out of my lips. Once have I sworn by my holiness that I will not lie unto David.

Psalms 89:34-35

The covenant simply means what God says, what God promised to do for his people that has a seal of God's oath, God's name, God's righteousness, and God's faithfulness on it as an assurance before the creations that such things must surely come to pass, a reality, a testimony, an event, and an experience among those that the promise was given to as their own inheritance in the kingdom of God.

In the book of Genesis ***chapter 22:15-18, "The word of God declares "And the angel of the Lord called unto Abraham out of heaven the second time and said, by myself have I sworn, saith the Lord, for because thou hast done this thing, and hast not withheld thy son, thine only son, that in blessing I will bless thee, and in multiplying, I will multiply thy seed as the stars of the heaven, and as thy sand which is upon the sea shore, and thy seed shall posses the gates of his enemies".***

God sworn by himself that by the virtue of his covenant that the descendants of father Abraham shall walk in the realities of manifold blessings of God in every generations, and possess without struggles the gates of their enemies.

By the virtue of salvation, you are a seed of Abraham, and the church has become the covenant nation emerging from the lineage of Abraham the founding father of our covenant with God, and our faith in Christ Jesus.

Even as Abraham believed God, and it was accounted to him for righteousness know ye therefore that they which are of faith the same are the children of Abraham. So then they which be of faith are blessed with faithful Abraham.

Galatians 3:6-7, 9

The covenant that God made with father Abraham is the covenant God made with the saints, and the church of Jesus Christ in every dispensation of grace. And one of the miracles that follow this covenant is that it cannot fail, it cannot be manipulated by the devil, and it cannot be restricted by the economy of nations both in seasons, and out of season.

By the virtue of the power of God that is backing this covenant you are ordained to live in royalty, to abide in prosperity, to walk in enviable success, and to enter into a world of financial liberty that gives no room for frustration, sorrow, losses, and crisis, and that is the place God is taking you to from today henceforth.

Friend, there shall be a confirmation of covenant of prosperity, and financial riches in your life.That is the word of promise from God for your life that has the seal of God's faithfulness on it.All you need to do is to believe that it is possible, and stand in the place of faith in your walk with God and you will see strange miracles taking place in your finances in all ramifications.

WONDERS OF OMNIPOTENT FAITH

Omni potent faith is the operations of faith that establishes the acts of God, the works of God, the promises of God, and the will of God, for the creations and the saints of God in affairs of nations to confirm the covenant of God among his people.

Child of God, this realm of faith is the realm of faith that is not open to mortals, only God, the divinity, the trinity, and all the agents of the supernatural, and the miraculous are allowed to walk in it.

Many people don't know that God is a faith God, God understands the language of faith, it takes the God who has faith to call the things that be not into existence, it takes the God who operates in the potent faith to say 'let there be light' in the beginning, and there was light.

When God is set to operate with his omnipotent faith, what you choose to believe or not to believe does not matter, what matters is that the integrity of his covenant, and his name must be confirmed and established among his people with open miraculous.

I am sent by God to tell the saints that there are some miracles, promises of God for them, supernatural experiences for you that cannot be a reality in this dispensation with their own level of faith, but God is already walking in this kind of faith to confirm his promises to the church in this dispensation of grace.

Say unto God, how terrible are thou in thy works, through the greatness of thy power shall thine enemies submit themselves unto thee. Come and see the works of God; he is terrible in his doings towards the children of men.

Psalms 66:3, 5

This is a new day, this is a new dispensation of grace, and this is an era of miraculous live never before. God will humble impossibilities at the feet of his saints, he will confirm the covenant of prosperity, and financial dominion in the body of Christ in this generation with open victory over the curse of the heathen against the welfare of the saints in the national heights of nations.

KEYS TO WALK IN THE COVENANT

1. Be a faith practicing believer
2. Believe in the acts of the miraculous.
3. Believe in the strange works of God
4. Believe that tithing covenant
5. Believe that giving covenant in the kingdom of God
6. Walk in fear of God without compromise
7. Believe in the testimonies of the prophets
8. Believe in service of God's house
9. Don't have any other alternative god or means of promotion
10. Live a faithful life, and uphold integrity in your relationship with men.
11. Stand in the integrity of the word of God in every situation and keep believing that the word of God cannot fail you, as you continue to hold unto God this way, a door shall open in heaven for you, and the word of God which is settled in heaven shall be vindicated in your life, and finances with outstanding miracles of success and prosperity.

CHAPTER 12

WISDOM OF SUPERNATURAL WEALTH

Supernatural wealth is a gift of God that answers to the operations of the wisdom of God. For you to be a man that will walk in the realities of supernatural wealth, you must be a man that is blessed with the wisdom of God.

Child of God, the wisdom of God is the gift of God that commands and attracts prosperity to answer to you without struggles. Whenyou will begin to walk in the overflowing prosperity, it is just a matter of time you will become a man that has a supernatural wealth as a blessing of God upon your life.

"A gift is as a precious stone in the eyes of him that hat it,
Withersoever it turneth, it prospereth".

Proverbs 17:8

The wisdom of God is a precious gift that attracts prosperity and supernatural wealth with struggles. We are in the days that the believers need to turn to wisdom of God to walk in the realities of wealth and riches that cannot be hindered or be frustrated by the economic of his world.

The day so severe hardship, bad economic, and financial crisis in the nations are also the days of God's power when the believers who knows their God shall command supernatural breakthrough and supernatural wealth by operating in the wisdom of God.

"Wisdom is the principal thing; therefore get wisdom;
And with all thy getting get understanding.
Exalt her, and she shall promote thee, she shall bring thee to honour,
When thou doest embrace her.
She shall give to thine head an ornament of grace, a crown of glory shall she deliver to thee".

Proverbs 4:7-9

The wisdom God is a treasure and a precious gift of God that attracts supernatural wealth without struggles, and as a child of God you need it to walk in the realities of supernatural wealth.

When the wisdom of God is at work in your life, the curses of poverty shall be broken byforce.Wealth and riches shall be created through your hands as a sign to witness that divine deposit of the spirit is upon your head.

We are in the days when the saints of God need to cry to God for wisdom, the believers need to tarry in the mountain of prayers to seek for God's wisdom.Wisdom is a precious gift of heaven that is ordain to break financial hardship and handover economic powers to the believers this end-time.

REALITIES OF THE WISDOM OF GOD

This wisdom of God is the divine empowerment, and deposit of the inspiration, creative power, understanding, knowledge of God that empowers the one that received it to walk into supernatural blessing in creating wealth, in achieving business prosperity, and living a victorious life of success over all the issues of life as a man empowered by God to have financial dominion.

Anywhere you see the wisdom of God at work in its fullness, just know that wealth and riches cannot lack there.Anywhere you see the wisdom of God at work in realities, it is a sign that the mantle of supernatural prosperity, success, breakthrough; and wealth creation has been released as a reality and as an operation of the spirit that will financial miracles that will be spoken after many generations as a sign that came to tabernacle in their midst.

"For wisdom is better than rabies; and all the things that may be
Desired are not to be compared to it, I wisdom dwell with prudence,
And find out knowledge of wealth involved by the kings reign,
And princes decree justice.
By me princes rule,
And noble even all the judges of the earth riches and honour are with me,
Yea, durable riches and righteousness.
Proverbs 8:11-12, 15-16

The wisdom of God is a precious endowment of God, it is a deposit of the Holy Ghost, and impartation from God; that empowers ordinary and poor men to rise up suddenly to become men that are wealth creators, and giant business men on earth.

When the flow of the spirit of wisdom is at work in your life, you breakthrough supernaturally into the realm of business.The inspiration to create possibilities in the midst of impossibility that have the upper hand in the financial and business system of this world shall be at work in your life.

KEYS TO RECEIVE THE WISDOM FOR SUPERNATURAL WEALTH FROM GOD

1. Walk in the fear of God
2. Be addicted lover of God
3. Live a righteous and holy life
4. Believe and practice financial covenant as a lifestyle
5. Be diligent in business
6. Be a regular tithe payer
7. Be cheerful;: and generous giver to support the work of God
8. Be hospitable to the need of the poor, the brethren, and the welfare of the house of God.
9. Uphold godly principles in your business pursuit
10. Be fervent in prayers and in your relationship with God
11. Walk in the realities of genuine salvation

SALVATION IS A GIFT OF GRACE

Salvation is a gift of grace that brought redemption blessing of Jesus Christ to us who are lost in sins and iniquity to express the love of God that is able to break the curses of sin upon your lives through the sacrifices of the lamb of God.

Salvation simply means freedom from sins, deliverance from the curses of Satan, and a release from the afflictions of poverty and condemnation of kingdom of darkness through the death of Jesus Christ that empowers you to have access to God's joy, what God labored for in his kingdom without restrictions, deprivation, is denial.

"For the grace of God that bringeth salvation hath appeared to all men.
Teaching us that deying ungodliness and worldly lust,
We should live soberly, righteously, and godly,
In this present world.

Titus 2:11-12

The grace of God brought salvation to you to break the yoke of sin, iniquity, ungodliness and worldliness in you so that you can walk in God as a consecrated believer worthy of praise, in the sight of God.

Where the grace of God is at work, you will see financial prosperity at work in that place, and where salvation of our Lord Jesus Christ is at work in you until realities of super natural blessing is at work in that place.

Child of God; one of the reasons salvation came to you is a break the curse of poverty in your life, and the reason why the grace of God came to abide in your life is to connect you to the unsearchable treasures and riches of God's inheritance among the saints including financial inheritance.

If you are not walking in the realities of genuine salvation, ask God to restore the profession of your faith for that is your spiritual blessing that empowers you to live a life without limitations, by the virtue of redemption, Christ has become your sufficiency in all things.

CHAPTER 13

WALKING IN FINANCIAL DOMINION

Financial dominion is a reality, it is not only a truth, it is also an experience that has existed among the faithful in the kingdom of God, and this experience is being subjected to a great awakening of God among the saints in this dispensation.

Financial dominion is a reality that is coming back as the occurrences of the supernatural among the saints of God in this generation.Many believers even in these hard times shall encounter the miracle of financial dominion in all field of life in unimaginable ways to the glory of God.

Is it not yet a little while, and Lebanon shall be turned into a fruitful field, and the fruitful field shall be esteemed as a forest. The meek also shall increase their joy in the Lord, and the poor among men shall rejoice in the Holy one of Israel.

Isaiah 29:17, 19

When the anointing for fruitfulness and productivity comes upon the saints of God, the outcome of it, shall be financial dominion. God is releasing the anointing for fruitfulness upon the poor among the saints, many people will rise up to overcome poverty like a dream of the night.

What is financial dominion? Financial dominion simply means to have authority over money, to have power over riches, and to have control over your economy in such a way that you afford a good life, a better standard of life, and meet your financial needs without any limitations or lack.

"For the Lord God is a sun and shield; the Lord will give grace and glory; no good thing will he withhold from them that walk uprightly".

Psalms 84:14

Financial dominion simply means to have availability of money in your life to solve problems for you at the time you want it, how you want it, and to a level you want your needs to be met.

Financial dominion simply means the money answering to your hand work, hard labour, business, and productivity in abundance, and with immeasurable profits in such a way that you lack nothing at all that money can afford, and any good thing that can be referred to as the blessings of God.

"Thus saith the Lord thy Redeemer, the Holy one of Israel, I am the Lord thy God which teacheth thee to profit, whichleadeth thee in the way thou shouldest go".

Isaiah 48:17

Child of God, salvation came to empower you to walk in the realities of financial dominion, and the realities of financial dominion is ordained by God to occur in your life with physical signs following to confirm it in your life.

REALITIES OF FINANCIAL DOMINION

Financial dominion is just a proclamation of faith among the believers, rather it is ordained to be the reality of every believer in Christ.

When financial dominion becomes your reality, the signs cannot be hidden, the signs will be open for everyone to see it that the blessings of God is upon your life.

SIGNS OF FINANCIAL DOMINION

Financial dominion is a sign ordained by God to follow you at the point of salvation, and the signs of financial dominion are as follows.

1. **CHANGE OF STATUS:** It is the will of God for you to have good befitting status as a believer, and live a life that shows that God has given you financial and economic power over your needs in life.

   Child of God, it is the will of God for you to be in a position where you afford good things of life, and good things that you desire in your work with God, and in the society, God ordained it to be, to make sure that you are not brought under mockery, shame, reproach in the public because of poverty. From today, there shall be a change of status for you, there shall be a change of level for you, and situations shall bow to you to the glory of God.

2. **CHANGE OF POSITION:** It is the will of God for you as a child of God to have a change of position, God wants you to have a good financial position in life.

In the books of Ecclesiastes chapter 10:6-7, the word of God says ***"Folly is set in great dignity, and the rich sit in low places! I have seen servants upon horses, and princes walking as servants upon the earth."***

There shall be a change of position in your life, suddenly, you shall live the place of poverty, suffering, joblessness, financial slavery to take your position in the seat of financial dominion for that is the position that is allotted to you as your inheritance in Christ.

Child of God, you are an heir of salvation, salvation adopted you to have a better financial story in life, salvation came to break the shackles of stubborn poverty, and financial slavery in your life. Anywhere that your financial position is being held bound under the contention and captivity of satan, wickedness, witches and wizards, principalities and powers there shall be a release, restriction, and recovery for you in a twinkle of an eye.

3. **ROYALTY AND KINGSHIP:** Royalty and kingship is your inheritance in Christ. Royalty and kingship in Christ is not a confession of faith only, rather it is ordained by God to the experience, life reality, and existing world of the saints.

   Child of God, by the virtue of redemption, you are born again to reign as kings with Christ, and live as a prince in the kingdom of God as your salvation experience.

   "But ye are a chosen generation, a royal priesthood, an holy nation, a peculiar people, that ye should show forth the praises of him who hath called you out of darkness into his marvellous light".

   1Peter 2:9

   As a believer, you are called to salvation to enjoy the privileges and opportunities that kings, queens, rulers, and princes enjoy in the palaces, in the nation, and in the society.

   Salvation is a reality, and the word of God is a sure reality, the promises of God are not God's wishes for you, rather they are God's completed miraculous works in your life.

   Based on this understanding, it is very obvious that God b the virtue of redemption option you to have class in the society in such a way that you will live in affluence, luxury, better life, and be in the position to afford precious things of life, and treasures as a prove that you came from a kingdom where money is not a problem and a kingdom where money is not rebellious against its master.

"He hath shown his people the power of his works, that he may give them the heritage of the heathen".

Psalms 111:6

God is changing your position in the society, God is restoring your royalty like in the days of the former, God is restoring your right of kingship with privileges like in the days of the later rain, and the testimony that will come out of it, is that you shall be repositioned and enthroned to have a place among the rich, the wealthy, and the elites in the society, and surely it must come to pass.

4. **OWNERSHIP:** Ownership is a sign of financial dominion ordained by God to follow your salvation as believer. Ownership simply means right given to you by God to have possessions, to have national wealth, and to worth treasures and precious things of life. According to the book of Proverb chapter 19:14 the word of God says ***"house and riches are the inheritance of a father."*** God takes pleasure in your achievement, than in your worthlessness, and emptiness.

   God wants you to be an owner of material possessions, and have an edge over material blessings, your poverty does not bring any glory of God until it is changed to be a condition that has faded away. From today, your poverty shall fade away, your worthlessness and emptiness shall fade away, your right of ownership be restored to the glory of God.

CHAPTER 14

PRINCIPLES OF SUCCESS FOR BELIEVERS

There is a call from the kingdom of God, God is calling the believers to return back to principles that controls success in the kingdom of God, for that is the keys that will open the doors of multiple success, and ever increasing progress for you in this era.

WHO ARE THE BELIEVERS?

The believers are the redeemed of the Lord, who are washed by the blood of the lamb, and have settled in the house of God has God's elect, and inheritance on the surface of the earth.

The believers are the saints of God who are begotten the word of God, whose profession of faith, and test, many in Christ has test, tried, and trusted with a prove that they are the faithful ones in the body of Christ whose walks with God is filled with assurance of the promises of God.

"Therefore, the redeemed of the LORD shall
Return and come with singing unto Zion;
And everlasting joy shall be upon their head; they shall obtain gladness
And joy, and sorrow and mourning shall fee away".
Isaiah 51:11

To era of divine visitation for the believers is now, many believers shall walk with success without struggles in this generation.

Child of God, success is the promise of God for the believers, success is the inheritance of the saints in this era, success is the portion of the redeemed in this generation but, the truth remains that you cannot get into a progressive and enduring success in the kingdom of God without operating with the principles of success that rules the kingdom of God that believers are ordained to uphold it as a key that will separate them from the people of this world as a peculiar people that is blessed by God.

The kingdom of God is a kingdom that is controlled by principles, and you cannot be a child of God without understanding the language of lasting success, without operating with the principles of success that controls the kingdom of God. The reason where many believers are far away from success while many are not experiencing lasting success because they want to succeed according worldly principles and mindset of civilization thereby despising the word of God.

WHAT IS A PRINCPLE? Principles are rules, ordinances of righteousness, laws, and code of code formed to control an actions, lifestyle, and someone else believe system in the course of life.

Without principles, you cannot live a life of success, a life that is filled with progress and focus on the pursuit of your personal goals, and visions as an individual. Every kingdom has their principles, individuals has their principles, and the kingdom has its principles that control success among the believers.

UNDERSTANDING KINGDOM PRINCIPLES

Kingdom principles are the keys of God's kingdom that is being handed over to the church, and to the believers to trade with it as a spiritual principles, and godly values in the pursuit of their destiny, success, business and endeavours in the world.

Kingdom principles are ordain as spiritual keys that can open the doors success, prosperity, and great in the pursuit of business vision for those who will choose to operate in obedience to the word of God.

"I know thy works, behold, I have set before thee an open doors,
And no man can shut it, for thou hast a little strength,
And hast kept my word, and hast not denied my name".

Revelation 3:8

Kingdom principles are ordained to open the doors of success for you as a believer, because they are the percepts and virtues that flows in the word of God to answereth the believers for kingdom order of success and godly prosperity and what is the essence of being a Christian if you are not thinking on how to be a blessing to the work of God? To the kingdom of God, and to every good works that glorifies God.

UNDERSTANDING SUPERNATURAL ELEVATION IN THE KINGDOM OF GOD

Supernatural elevation in the kingdom of God is the promise of God for a believer, but the truth is that for you to walk in the realities of supernatural elevation you have to pay attention to the principles of God's kingdom.

Many believers are not enjoying supernatural elevation in the pursuit of their endeavours because they have forsaken the principles of Gods kingdom, and have close worldly principles as a ladder to get to the top.

"Show me thy ways, O LORD, teach me thy paths.
Lead me in thy truth, and teach me for thou art the God of my salvation on Thee do I wait all the day".

Psalms 25:4-5.

Supernatural elevation is a promise of God for you as a child of God, but kingdom principles are like keys that you to operate with to see the reality of that promise.

Supernatural elevation is a blessing of upliftment in buses, visions, dreams and aspirations of life that is obtainable with your obedience to the principles of God's kingdom.

As you cannot open the door with a wrong keys that is the same you cannot open the doors of supernatural elevation by applying worldly principles. As it takes the right keys to open a door that is the same it takes applying kingdom principles to climb the ladder of supernatural elevations in the pursuit of success in your endeavours as a child of God.

EXPLORING 14 PRINCIPLES OF SUCCESS FOR BELIEVERS

1. **FIRST LOVE FOR GOD:** Loving God the first love in your heart is the principles that leads to success, according to the first commandment you are under obligation to love God first before any other thing.

   Child of God, to love God first before any other thing is to put God first in your life, finances, business, and endeavours with responsibility that you have seek the righteousness of God in truth and spirit, and seek the interest of God's kingdom first by dedicating all you have, all that God blessed you with to support the work of God according to the book of Matthew 6:33.

2. **HOLINESS:** In the book of Psalms Chapter 1:1 the word of God says ***"Blessed is the man that walketh not in the counsel of the ungodly, nor standeth in the way of sinners, nor sitteth in the seat of scornful".***

Holiness is the key that can open many doors of success for you in the kingdom of God, when sin is overcomed in your life it creates opportunity for the blessing to flow to you in dimensions. When the siege of sinful habits is broken in your life, it attracts the goodwill of men, and people to you, because of the presence of God that men will notice upon your life, they will be eager to draw nearer to you to bless you according to the prompting of the spirit.

Holiness is a value in the kingdom of God that can cause many doors of success to open to you, because holiness is the attitude of the spirit and every fruit of the spirit is ordained for your separation from worldliness, and when worldliness is destroyed in your life, supernatural blessings shall be a reality.

3. **CONSECRATION TO GOD'S PURPOSE:** Consecration simply means an act of separating yourself from sins and worldliness to dedicate yourself and your life as a sanctified vessels made available to be used by God.

What is the essence of your success, and prosperity, and financial blessings when it cannot be used by God, what is the essence of being a Christian if you are not thinking on how to be blessing to the work of God, to the kingdom of God, and to every good works that glorifies God.

Child of God, God does not do anything without a purpose, every success and prosperity in the kingdom of God given to you are ordain to serve the purpose of God among the brethren for you to walk I n the realities of supernatural success and prosperity you must consecrate yourself to God's purpose to use your life, your business, your financial, your gifts, your success and prosperity to serve God.

When a believer came into this realm and understanding he has adopted a principles of success in the kingdom of God that will make sure that everything is walking together for you according to God's purpose as it is written in the book of Romans 8:28.

4. **OBEDIENCE TO GOD'S WORD:** Decisions to live an obedient life in your Christian faith to the word of God is a kingdom principles that attracts supernatural success to you. When you begin to uphold the counsel of God's word in obedience, you will become a believer that God will be appointed unto favour, goodness, and mercy before men, and before kings to help you until you get to the top.

The believers are not seeing in the realities of supernatural success in a dimension that it supposed to flowing among the saints according to the covenant, because many believers have become hearers of the word, and not doers of the word.

"But be ye doers of the word, and not hearers only, only, deceiving your own selves. For if any be a hearers of the word, and not a doer, he is like unto a man beholding his natural face in a glass.
For hebeholdeth himself, and goeth his way, and straight way
Forgeteth what manner of man he was.
But whose looketh into the perfect law of liberty and
Continueth therein; in being not a forgetful hearer,
But a doer of the work, this man shall be blessed in his deed
James 1:22-25

Obedience to God's word is to be a doer of God's word, it means to be a man that live your life according to the defects, instructions, ordinances, and counsel of God world, when that becomes your lifestyle, and your passion and your habit supernatural success will win towards you to embrace your daily.

5. **DEMOSTRATION OF FAITH:** Faith is to believe what God says, to do what the word of God says, and act on what God told you to do in his word according to the dimension of truth, light, revelation and voice of God that came through the instruction of the Holy Spirit.

In the book of James Chapter 2:14, the Bible says "What do it profit, my brethren though a man say he hath faith and have not works? Can faith save him?

Demonstration of faith simply means expression of you faith, and the application of your faith on God in line with the word of God that is revealed to you in any issues of life, believing God to confirm it with desired expectations.

Child of God, you can be a product of supernatural success and prosperity until you become a man that walks in faith with God.Taking the step of faith in the pursuit of your endeavours that gives no room to any form doubts, compromise, or rebellion to the word of God, when you begin to uphold it as your life principle, success is inevitable in your life expectations.

6. **DEDICATION TO BUSINESS:** Business boom is a promise and a blessing of God for every believer, but the big truth is that business prosperity, success and achievement cannot happen by wishes, by luck alone, rather it is a product of hard work, commitment, dedication and your drive in life.

   It is the will of God for you, dedicate yourself to your business as one of your principles, for whatever you give to life, is what life will bring back to you in return. In the book of Proverbs ***Chapter 22:29, the word of God says; "Seest thou a man diligent in his business?He shall stand before kings, he shall not stand before mean men".***

   Do you desire to stand before kings, dedicate yourself to your business,labour in that business until your labour begin to yield streams of income and profit for you.

   The promises of God does not answer to idle people, it answers to hardworking believers, you need to uphold dedication to business as one of your principles of success, as a child of the kingdom, and the outcome of it shall be a fruitful testimony.

7. **INTEGRITY:** Integrity is a virtue that propels a man to stand upright before God, and before men in the fear of the Lord. Many believers have come to place of breakthrough and was deprived promotions by God because there is no uprightness, no integrity, and the fear of God in your lives, as your principles.

Let integrity become your watch-ward because it is like a candle light that enlights your world to be free from the attacks of failure, let uprightness be the girdle of your loins for it is like lamb that chases darkness away from your destiny, as a child of God.

When you begin to live a life of integrity in your walk with God, success will bow to you and prosperity will embrace and supernatural doors will open for you in their own accord.

8. **FAITHFULNESS:** Faithfulness is an act of being trustworthy, because of your stand for truth, honesty, and openness, and fairness in your relationship with God, and with men in the secret places, and in the public.

Honest men are disappearing in the scene in this generation, as a child of God you need to step into that position to full that vacuum, men of integrity are disappearing in the society. As a believer, you need to step into that position to fill that vacuum for it comes the savior of grace, the smells of favour, and the oil of mercy that distinguish a man among his colleagues in the business field.

"Examine me, O LORD, and prove me, try my reins and
My heart. I have not sat with vain persons,
Neither will I go in with dissamblers. I have hated the congregations
Of evil doers, and will not sit with the wicked.
I will wash mine hands in innocence; so will I compass thine altar,
O Lord".

Psalm 26:2, 4-6

Faithfulness is important in this dispensation, God cannot entrust the treasures and riches of his kingdom into the hands of unfaithful people or believers. Men that will control the precious things of God's kingdom in this dispensation of grace are men whose life are prompted by fire to live in honesty.

9. **TITHING AND SELFLESS FINANCIAL SACRIFICES:** Tithing and selfless financial sacrifices is a principle in the kingdom of God that leads to success and prosperity.

Tithing is a practice of the covenant, and financial sacrifices is kingdom commandment that makes a prosperous man out of a struggling man.

"But this I say, he which soweth sparingly shall reap also sparingly,
And he which soweth bountifully shall reap also bountifully
2Corinthians 9:6

Selfless financial sacrifices are the keys to unlock your doors of financial breakthrough, while tithing is ordained to keep the confirmation of the covenant of wealth at work in your finances, and business as a reality that connects fail, neither can it be hidden.

10. **HUMILITY:** In the book of 1Peter 5:5c to the word of God says *"God resisteth the proud, and giveth grace to the humble? "Humble yourselves therefore under the mighty hand of God, that he may exalt you in due time.*

11. **PATIENCE:** Patience is a precious virtue in the kingdom of God, it is a value that nobody want to covert in the christiandom, many believers are in haste to touch the blessings in the walk with God, without knowing that quick blessings is a promise of God for the saints, but waiting patiently upon God to the blessing to come is a test of the spirit that you must go through to prove to God that you lean on him in every situation.

"I waited patiently for the Lord, and he inclined unto me,
And heard my cry. He brought me up also out of an
Horrible pit, out of the miry clay, and set my feet upon a rock,
And established my goings.
Psalms 40:1

Patience is a great virtue in the kingdom of God that you must covert as your principle, and when it becomes your principle, it will lead you to touch the deep blessings of God that is free from sorrow and frustrations.

12. **CONTENTMENT:** Contentment is the attributes of being satisfied with blessings of God in your life, some believers cannot be satisfied though matter how God blesses them because they are not living a contented life as a habit.

Many believers that God has blessed are not contented with the level of success and prosperity that God blessed them with because of their lust for worldly wealth has led them astray to greatness and covetousness.

To believe God for more blessing is not a sin but to live a life of greediness and covetousness, and lack of satisfaction to what God has blessed you already is a sin before God, and against yourself.

God is admonishing you to embrace contentment as one of your principles because it is ordain to bring you into satisfaction with what God has already done in your life.

13. **DEVOTION TO SERVICE:** Devotion to service simply means to dedicate your time, energy, resources, and life to selfless service to God, to humanity and to your generation.

Upholding kingdom service as one your principle in the pursuit of success is the key to unlock the doors of greatness, promotion, wealth and riches, and uncommon upon your life and your business.

When devotion to service becomes your lifestyle gates shall be opened unto you, greatness shall bow to you, and your generation shall celebrate you as a God sent among them.

14. **THANKSGIVING:** It is written in the word of God in everything that you give God thanksgiving, maintain lifestyle of thanksgiving as a daily habit in the pursuit of your vision and dreams, irrespective of the challenges that you a facing, avoid murmuring, bitterness, sadness and complains, to uphold thanksgiving and gratitude unto the Lord in everything that you do in life.

Thanksgiving is the key that attracts the presence of God, his right of countenance, and his person to follow you, and tabernacle with you as a support to your visions, and your welfare.

CHAPTER 15

MIRACLES IN THE FOLD OF FRUSTRATED BUSINESS MEN

There shall be miracles in the fold of frustrated business men, many of them who are shut up in the plague of bad economy never to raise their heads again in business shall experience supernatural turnaround in their business pursuits.

WHO ARE THIS FRUSTRATED BUSINESS MEN?

Friend, frustrated business men are business men who tasted the testimonies and realities of prosperity in the walk with God, but recently that prosperity is no longer with them, they have lost it as a result of financial crisis.

Frustrated business are people men who walked with God in their business and received the promise of business boom in reality.But as of today, they have lost the business prosperity, and men whose financial testimonies in their walk with God is shaking as a result of situation beyond their control that came upon them.

Frustrated business men are business men who are once rich, prosperous, wealthy in their business and finances because God blessed them, but as of today they have lost the reaches of financial blessings, and prosperity in their life as believers.

"I will declare the decree, the LORD hath said unto me,
Thou are my son, this day have I begotten thee.
Ask of me, and I shall give thee the heathen for thine Inheritance,
And the uttermost parts of the earth for thy possessions.
Psalms 2:7-8

Frustrated businessmen are business men who are fallen down in business to the extent that in the human eyes, there is no rising up for them, but in the kingdom of God there is rising up for them if there is failure, and falling down, there shall also be a bouncing back.

Frustrated businessmen are business men who are whose capital, investment, and profit lines were destroyed, altered, and closed by the wicked through the weapon of natural occurrences, surely the shall be a deliverance for them

MYSTERIES OF FINANCIAL DELIVERANCE

Financial deliverance is a reality, a supernatural occurrence, and a mystery in the kingdom of God.

When a financial blessings of a man comes under distribution, attacks, and oppressions of the devil, and the wicked what that man needs at that moment is financial deliverance from God. Financial deliverance is not the same thing with financial restoration, financial restoration is the return what was lost and stolen to the rightful person. Financial deliverance is to fight, delay and deal with powers that attacks the blessing and destroyed the blessings in the lives of the owner.

"He hath swallowed down riches, and he shall vomit them up again, God shall cast them out of his belly

Job 20:15

There shall be financial deliverance in the lives of frustrated business men, many of them shall experience financial restoration.

There shall be a roaring of creeping in the camp of the devil because whatever that has attacked your business, your prosperity, blessings in Christ shall be properly destroyed physically, spiritually, and materially your business shall be restored according to the glory of the former, and the glory of the latter rain.

"God thundereth marvelously with the voice of his excellency, And he will not stay them when his voice is heard.

Job 37:5

Financial deliverance is the marvelous, and wonderful works of God in the lives of his people who are suffering all manner of attacks both physically and spiritually in the finances, and in their business.

When financial deliverance is engaged by God, miracles do happen, restoration will take place, recovery is being impossible, and the word of is being vindicated with testimonies that proves God to be a living reality of prosperity among his faithful ones and covenant people.

BREAKING THE YOKES OF FINANCIAL CURSES

Financial deliverance is the mysterious works of God that break financial curses in the lives of his people. Is any financial curses that is formerly your life and the works of your hands, it is broken today in the name of Jesus Christ.

Is any way that the devil, the wicked, witches and wicked, and diabolic powers that laid a curse of failure, bad luck, losses, crisis, and poverty upon your life, and upon your business. It shall be destroyed today by the power of the Holy Ghost.

"For there is hope of tree, if it be cut down,
That it will sprout again, and that the tender branch thereof will not cease
Though the root thereof was old in the earth,
And the stock there of die in the ground.
Yet through the scent of water it will bud, and bring forth boughs
Like a plant.

Job 14:7-9

If the forces that is beyond your control has succeeded in destroying your business, capital, and your finances through diabolic powers, diabolic curses, and afflictions of the devil, that curse is broken today in the name of Jesus Christ.

THIS IS THE DAYS OF GOD'S POWER

The day of God's power is the day of vengeance, the day that God shall execute vengeance upon the powers afflicting the financial blessings of God's people. The days of God's power is the day that God will vindicate the prayers of the saints upon the wicked that has spoiled their inheritance among the nations.

The days of God's power is the day that impossibilities shall be made possible, and everything that you lost shall be recovered back to you in your business and finances.

The days of God's power is the day God in his infinite mercy shall reveal, confirm, and validate the testimonies of the word of God, and the covenant in the affairs of his people, and in their financial welfare among the nations.

POWER OF ECONOMIC LIBERATION

Economic liberation is also a personal experience, atimes God can overlook the economy of a nation, to bless the business of his people. There shall be economic liberation again in the camp and affairs of the saints in this dispensation for that is one of the testimony of the covenant that God will confirm among the believers.

WHAT IS ECONOMIC LIBERATION

Economic liberation is occurrences of the supernatural in the financial affairs of the world, the nations, cities, with the purpose of making life easy for the people, and the forsake of making business profitable again for the benefit of the masses.

Economic liberation is also a personal experience, atimes God can overlook the economy of a nation, to bless the business of his people in such a way that they will have economic power to afford good life, and to prosper in their endeavours to confirm the promises of his word which they have come to believers by faith.

Personally you shall walk in the realities of economic liberation because the same way God takes pleasure in the economic prosperity that is the same way God takes pleasure in your own financial prosperity, because it is the benefit of it. If the economy of a nation is prosperity, and you are not prospering, where is your blessing when your country is prospering, and you are not prospering, which means that as a Christian the source of your prosperity is not the economy of your prosperity is not the economy of your country, rather the source of your prosperity is God whether the economy is bad or good.

"Save now, I beseech thee, O LORD;
O LORD, I beseech thee, send now prosperity".

Psalms 118:25

God is sending prosperity to your life, your finances, and your business, receive it with seven folds "amen". For it must surely come to pass in your life without delay from today henceforth.

If your business is folding up, and you are at the point of being disgraced in business by your debtors, there shall be a miracle happening in your life in that situation.

If you are at the point of losing your business as a result of financial crisis, and business commitments that did not work well with you, there shall be miracle of deliverance happening in your direction to see you from shame in the name of Jesus Christ.

CHAPTER 16

MONEY SHALL BE YOUR SLAVE

In the book of Ecclesiastes Chapter 10:19 the word of God says *"A feast is made for laughter, and wine maketh merry, but money answereth all things".*

Money answereth all things simple means that money is important in the human life, and the welfare of the human race. Money is ordained in the human realm to be a problem solver, in the affairs of mankind.

Child of God, if money is important in the survival of the human race, it means that money is also vital in the survival of the saints of God in this world.

But the higher birth realms that what is not given the power, authority, influence to control your welfare as a believer, because it is not the will of God for you to be enslaved by the provision and availability of money.

The will of God for your life is that Christian that will live beyond the control of money, and to be in control money in such a way that money will be humbled to serve you, to obey, and to work for you, and be at your service without rebelling against your authority.

"What is man, that thou art mindful of him and the son of man,
That thou visitest him? For thou hast made him a little lower than angels,
And hast crowned him with glory and honour.
Thou made me o have dominion over the works of thy hands,
Thou hast put all things under his feet".

Psalms 8:4-6

God created you to have dominion over all things by the value of creation, but by the virtue of salvation, God called you into sonship in his kingdom to have authority, control and power over money in reality, and in your daily life in such a way money shall as a servant, and as a slave to you to confirm the promise of abundance that God promised you in his life.

WHAT DOES IT MEAN FOR MONEY TO BE YOUR SLAVE

Money to be your slave simply means that money will answer to your needs, desires, and petitions and be available at your service in abundant ways.

Money to be your slave as a child of God, simply means to live a life without poverty, lack, want, because money is flowing to you as a divine provision and supplies in immeasurable ways.

Money to be your slave as a child of God simply means you walking in the realities of riches, wealth, sufficiency, prosperity, and deep success in such aaway that money is not a problem in your life for a lifetime.

Child of God, may I let you know that as kings of the earth reigns, money in the kingdom, that is the same way the saints are called by God into kingship and royalty to reign on earth with money in the kingdom of God.

You are not called to salvation to be slave to money, rather you are called to salvation for money to be your slave. You are not called by salvation to loose your voices as a result of lack of money, rather you are called into salvation to have a voice over money.

Infant, one of the signs that should follow you as a child of God through the salvation of our Lord Jesus Christ is the circulation, and availability of money in your direction

"According to his divine power hath given unto us all things that pertain Unto life and godliness through the knowledge of him that hath called us to glory and virtue.

2Peter 1:3

God is changing your relationship with money, God is humbling the pride of money against the saints in this generation, God is subjecting money to sever the saints, while the people of God will be in control of money in their affairs to confirm the covenant of wealth that God gave the believers through the finished works of salvation.

CONTROLLING THE FLOW OF MONEY

Money shall came under your control, riches and wealth shall be at you service, prosperity shall be not the far away from you, and success will be your life time testimonies.

It is the verdict of the covenant to make money what you will not be struggling for it before you get, it is the will of God to make money what you will not be praying for before you get it.It is the promise of God to make money what you will not begging for it to come to you because according to the principles of the covenant, money is ordained to flow to you, to come, your direction as a believer out of season and in season to confirm that you are called to salvation to have all sufficiency that God gave to the saints in Christ.

SECOND CHANCE TO PROVE GOD

There is a great reconciliation carried to take place among God's people, God is bringing the believers to place of reconciliation of peace, reconciliation of faith, and reconciliation of obedience to his biblical commandment.

"Good and upright is the LORD, therefore will he teach sinners
In the way. The meek will he guide in judgment;
And the meek will he teach his way"

Psalms 25:8-9

Second chance to prove God an administration to try God again, to hold unto God's word again, to dwell on God's promises again in your Christian without wavering, doubts, and slumbering in your wealth, and in your walk with God.

We are living in the days that the power of God is made of none effect by the backsliding of many believers, many believers are loosing confidence on the promises of god because severe trials, while many have lost their faith in their walk with God because of financial challenges, and economic problems.

Child of God, it is time to prove God again, it is time to give God chance again to revive your faith afresh in order to reveal his power in your life in the area of your financial needs. To prove God the second time is the act of faith that propels you to return back to covenant practices of God's word that commits you to begin take responsibility in obeying the word of God without compromising, with hypocrisy, without wavering, in your financial dealings with God, when this is done properly you will discover that God will reconcile you again to the flow of financial blessings in this kingdom.

"I will be glad and rejoice in thy mercy for thou has considered my troubles;
Thou hast known my soul in adversities let me not be ashamed,
O Lord, for I have called upon thee, let the wicked be ashamed, and let them silent in the grave".

Psalms 31:7, 17

The hour for you to renew your faith on the promises of God afresh has come, and the time for you to renew and dedicate your complete obedience to the word of god in your financial matters and dealing with God is now.

Child of God, you need to prove God again now that your tithing, giving practices, and financial dedication to the welfare of God's house, God's kingdom, and to the work of God in this dispensation because that is a requirement to open your financial doors in such a way that money cannot have authority over you.

"Bring ye all the tithes into the storehouse,
That there may be meat in mine house, and prove me now herewith,
Saith the LORD of hosts, if I will not open you the windows of heaven,
And pour you out a blessing, that there shall be no room enough
To receive It".

Malachi 3:11

According to this scripture, God said that you should prove him, God is calling him to put him to test, God is challenging you to try him with your obedience to tithe giving, alms giving, offering, and financial service to his kingdom.

God is challenging you to test his power to see regain and see whatever the miraculous will not answer to you in your financial request, and expectations from heaven.

The reason why many believers are walking in severe hardship, crisis, calamity, suffering, deprivation in the finances is because they are not faithful to God in tithing, in giving, in offering, and them financial commitment in the house of God, in the kingdom of God, and to the work of God.

BREAKING CURSES OF CLOSED HEAVEN

Many believers are labouring under a closed heaven, and when your heaven is closed where your blessing will come from.

Many believers are laboring under a closed heaven not because of their sins, but because of their disobedient to tithing covenant, and every disobedient no matter how spiritual it may be, it is a sin before the Lord.

Rebellion against God in paying your tithes is not just a sin against God, it is also a sin against the covenant, against the word of God, and against the church of Jesus Christ that God handled over the ordinances and commandments to watch over it to keep it and to watch over you to obey it.

"Will a man rob God? Yet ye have robbed me,
But ye say, wherein have we robbed thee? In tithes and offering
Ye are cursed with a curse, for ye have robbed me, even tithes and offering".
Malachi 3:8-9

When a sin last for a long time, it will become a harden heart against the ordinances of God and such sin will attract a closed heaven in the life of a believer.

God is calling you to repentance, turn away from your rebellion against the tithing covenant, for that is what you need to pull your business, finances, back of your hands, and your prayers out of the curses and plague of closed heavens in this dispensation.

God is not a man when you meet the requirement of the covenant, he will prove to you that his faithfulness faileth not at all times, in every generation, and in every dispensation that comes to serve the saints.

If your heaven is closed, the time for God to open it for you has come. F you are laboring and trading under a closed heaven, the time for you to begin labour under open heaven has come for that is a promise from God.

OPENING THE WINDOWS OF HEAVEN

The windows of heaven is open upon your life, and God shall pour down his blessings upon your life for your financial recovery and restoration.

When the windows of heaven is open, your life, the signs that will follow you will financially recover, business boom restoration, ever-increasing business growth, multiplication and increase in your finances.

When the windows of heaven is open in your life inspiration for prosperity will be made available to you, and opportunity to regain what was lost, and flow in the streams of income, and profit shall be restored back to your life, business, and finances.

"Ye, the LORD will answer and say unto his people,
Behold, I will send you corn, and wine, and oil, and ye shall be satisfied
Therewith; and I will no more make you reproach among the heathen
Be glad then, ye children of Zion, and rejoice in the Lord your God,
For he hath given you the former rain moderately,
And he will cause, to come down for you the rain, the former rain,

And the latter rain in the first month

Joel 2:19, 13

The raining of financial blessing is coming back, because the windows of heaven are ready to open upon the saints. The rain of stress free prosperity and sudden success is coming down upon the people of God because windows of heaven is already opened out for a blessing.

The rain of business boom, riches and wealth is pouring forth upon the covenant practices in the house of god because windows of heaven is opened to pour forth the riches of financial blessings upon them as a fulfillment of Gods covenant upon his faithful ones.

Child of God, windows of heaven is already opened, but you need to connect to it, you need to tap into it to come into the realm of prosperity that God is opening to the blessing in this dispensation of grace. When your obedience is tested and trusted by God, they shall be a reward, and money shall bow to you in all ramifications.

CHAPTER 17

ANOINTING THAT BREEDS MILLIONAIRES AND BILLIONAIRES

There is anointing ordained by God to breed millionaires and billionaires in the body of Christ with a mandate from, nature and equip the believers who want to be in control of kingdom wealth in this dispensation to submit themselves under the regulations of kingdom principles.

To be blessed by God is a promise of God for every believer, and to walk in the realities of financial blessings is the inheritance of the saints in the salvation of our Lord Jesus Christ, but to become a man who is in control of kingdom wealth and riches comes with certain responsibilities and obligations that are there to bind you to the principles that controls covenant wealth and riches in the word of God.

But thou shalt remember the Lord thy God; for it is he that giveth thee power to get wealth, that he may establish his covenant which he sware unto thy fathers as it is this day.
Deuteronomy 8:18

Child of God, according to this scripture, the power to get wealth is from God, and the wealth itself comes from God. Until you are empowered to control wealth in the kingdom of God, wealth cannot flow to you.

The book of Deuteronomy 8:18 stated that there is a dimension of power in the covenant that empowers men to become rich, and wealth, and this power simply means the following:

1. The seal of the word of God
2. The mysteries of the kingdom
3. The terms of material blessings
4. The seal of the covenant
5. The operations of the Holy Ghost
6. The knowledge of God
7. The adoption into son-ship
8. The virtue of salvation
9. The application of faith
10. The practice of dominion

11. Devotion to God
12. Obedience to kingdom investment
13. Obedience to the ordinances of Christ
14. The operations of the anointing
15. The mysteries of supernatural wisdom

Child of God, these fifteen mysteries are ordained by God to lead you to covenant of wealth and riches, when they are properly engaged by the saints. The covenant of riches and wealth will be confirmed in the heavens to have realities among the believers on the surface of the earth without delays.

Based on this understanding, it is very clear that covenant wealth and riches cannot happen just by wishes, it can only happen through proper engagement with the manifold practices of the ordinances of the covenant in the kingdom of God.

"For God is the king of old, working salvation in the midst of the Earth. Have respect unto the covenant; for the dark Places of the earth are full of the habitation of the cruelty".

Psalms 74:12, 20

There is anointing that breeds millionaires and billionaires, and that anointing is ordained to reveal the manifold principles that controls wealth and riches in the kingdom of God with a mandate to lead the saints to financial breakthrough and prosperity that is able to create wealth and riches in the body of Christ.

Child of God, God is bringing this dimension of anointing afresh again to the church of Jesus Christ this end-time, many poor believers whose background has not stake in prosperity shall rise among nations to walk in the realities of covenant wealth and riches in this dispensation.

TAP INTO ANOINTING FOR PROSPERITY

There is a flowing oil ordained to connect you to kingdom prosperity, and this oil is an anointing oil ordained to flow from the altar in the house of God through the hand of the servant of God to raise millionaires and billionaires from the body of Christ.

Child of God, don't despise the efficacy of the anointing because it contains the deposit of the holy spirit ordained to break the curse of poverty upon your life, and raise you up to walk in financial blessings.

The anointing for prosperity contains the gifts of God that empowers men supernaturally to overcome poverty, and to create wealth out of nothing, and from the crash to the top.

Anointing for prosperity contains the consecration of the spirit that is ordained to set the believers apart to penetrate the realms of millionaires and billionaires as Godly people through the operations of the kingdom and covenant practices.

"I said unto the fools, deal not foolishly, and to the wicked, lift not up the horn; lift not up your horn on high, speak not with a stiff neck. For promotion cometh neither from the east, nor from the west, nor from the south. But God is the judge; he putteth down one, and setteth up another".

Psalms 75:4-7

The anointing oil is one of the mysteries of the Holy Ghost in the kingdom of God that contains the deposit of prosperity, success, financial blessing, and financial liberty ordained to break the shackles of ancient curses of poverty upon the saints through the ministration of servants of God consecrated for such purpose.

Child of God, is poverty tormenting you like a plague, you need to tap into the anointing for prosperity, are you tired of suffering financial hardship, frustrations, crisis and limitations in your life, pursuit, and destiny what you need is the anointing for prosperity.

When this anointing comes upon you not just as a ministration of a servant of God, but also as a grace of God upon your life, business, and life pursuit will become fruitful, and begin to yield unlimited profits for you.

POWER OF SPIRITUAL BLESSINGS

The anointing for prosperity is a ministration ordained to flow as a spiritual blessing upon the saints which has the capacity to create financial wealth and riches for the people of God.

Every spiritual blessing in the kingdom of God contains a creative power, creative virtue, and creative unction that can produce material wealth to the glory of God.

Blessed be the God and father of our Lord Jesus Christ, who hath blessed us with all spiritual blessings, in the heavenly places in Christ.

Ephesians 1:3

Spiritual blessings are precious gifts and treasures in the kingdom which values are more than the values of material blessings. When you begin to walk in realities of spiritual blessings of God as a child of God, one of the signs that should follow you is material blessing that attracts money to bow to you in your endeavours, and in your walk with God.

MATERIAL BLESSINGS SHALL BOW TO THE BELIEVERS THIS END-TIME

In the book of Deuteronomy ***chapter 28:8, 10,the word of God declares "The Lord shall command the blessing upon thee in thy storehouses, and in all that thou setest thine hand unto, and he shall bless thee in the land which the Lord thy God giveth thee. And all people of the earth shall see that thou art called by the name of the Lord; and they shall be afraid of thee."***

The believers by the virtue of ordination, are going to walk in fearful material blessings this end-time, there is a prosperity boom and festival coming like a cloud of the sun, and the morning to the body of Christ, shall overtake the glory of the former, and establish the latter rain prosperity in the church of Jesus Christ this end-time.

This prosperity boom will make the poor rich, and make the rejected to become the corner stone among the nations, many believers shall arise in the streets of the nations to celebrate the prosperity visitations of God in the cloud of the church before in the history of the church, and the kind of this visitation of God among his people shall produce righteousness among the saints in the affairs of the nations.

CHAPTER 18

PURPOSE OF SUPERNATURAL FAVOUR

God is the God of purpose, he does not do anything without a purpose, God called you to his eternal purpose to walk in the realities of supernatural favour.

WHAT IS FAVOUR?

Favour is the manifold works of God that enhances the life of a believer to live a life without struggles, toiling, and without hard labour.

Favour is the unlimited grace of God ordained to give a believer access to the manifold goodness and loving kindness of God to achieve things at ease, and to rise in life without much process, or protocols.

Favour is the seal of divine recommendation and approval of God upon a believer that can force closed doors to open before a man, make unimaginable miracles to happen to you in hard situations, and cause possibilities to occur I your life in the hard times.

I entreat thy favour with my whole heart; be merciful unto me according to thy word.

Psalms 119:58

Favour has a voice when it begins to speak for you, protocols are broken, and processes are withheld for you to rise in to unmerited success and prosperity. The hour that favour will speak for you has come, favour will be on your side again to build up your broken walls, and to mend the broken bridges of your life and your destiny.

Favour flows like a river, when it begins to flow in your life, difficulties are broken, and every siege of enslavement that made you a man without livelihood and stable source of survival will fall at your feet.

Child of God, when the smells of favour ceases to follow you, the flow of money will cease to be your reality, and the circulation of money will begin to pass you by in your daily existence, that is the reason why many believers are laid low financially in this dispensation, but the good news is that God is awakening supernatural favour to work for your good, and to rest upon the works of your hands, for you success to happen and appear without sorrow.

UNDERSTANDING SUPERNATURAL FAVOUR

Supernatural favour is a divine favour that comes from God and from the strange works of God. It is a dimension of favour that is not man-made, rather it is a favour from God.

Supernatural favour is the dimension of favour that is not limited in solving promises, and is powerless in terminating the enslavement of financial problems in your life, and upon the works of your hands.

When supernatural favour comes to play a role in your existence, dreams, riches will answer to you from the higher mountains of nations, and wealth will run towards you to embrace you.

Child of God, supernatural favour is a dimension of favour that raves the poor from the ground, to set him on a seat of success and prosperity has a man whom God has blessed.

How excellent is thy loving kindness, O God! therefore the children of men put their trust under the shadow of thy wings.
They shall be abundantly satisfied with the fullness of thy house, and thou shalt make them to drink of the rivers of thy pleasures.
Psalms 36:7-8

There is a release of favour upon your life that favour is supernatural favour, there is fresh outpouring of favour upon the works of your hands, that favour will speak and it cannot lie.

When supernatural favour is playing a role in your life, your access to success and prosperity cannot be restricted, or be hindered by natural powers, or opposing circumstances. When supernatural favour is at work in your business hard luck, bad luck, and lack of money will bow to you for financial blessing to become your reality.

FAVOUR WILL FOLLOW YOU AS A SIGN

Favour shall begin to follow you as a sign from today, from this moment, the thick cloud of failure, and anti-favour life experience is fading away in your life says the spirit of God.

When favour begins to follow you as a sign, miracles happens in their own accord in your life, and doors of unusual prosperity will open in their accord in your life.

As a redeemed child of God, it is not permitted for bad luck and hard luck to follow you, or to hang around your business activities. As a covenant child of God, it is not allowed for lack of money and scarcity of money to hang around you like an oppression of the devil, and like a monitoring spirit.

As a believer, who is begotten into the family of Jesus Christ, one of the signs that is ordained to follow you is favour that occurs in unusual manner, in a strange way, and in unpredicted ways.

"Behold, I and the children whom the Lord
Hath given me are for signs and for wonders in Isreal
From the Lord of hosts, which dwelleth in mount zion".

Isaiah 8:18

Favour is a sign that is appointed by God to follow you and to follow your destiny, when supernatural favour is follow you as a sign life becomes meaningful, your existence become desirable, and the works with your hands, and your destiny will be filled with the fruit of prosperity, and thanksgiving all the days of your life.

Child of God, a sign is the reflection of the miraculousand the supernatural in the affairs of the believers, and in the affairs of covenant people of God.

A sign is not an hidden thing when it is at work people will know, you will notice it, and its presence in your life will have proofs to show that is working for you.Favour is not a hidden thing because favour is a sign commanded by God to follow you, If it is not at work in your life, many things will go wrong in your destiny and events will be happening as if life is against you.

HEANDLING REASONS THAT CAN WITHHELD SUPERNATURAL FAVOUR IN YOUR LIFE

WHEN GOD HIDES HIS FACE: Supernatural favour can be withheld in your life when God is hiding his face from you and sin and iniquity is the reason why God can hide his face never to show you his right of countenance and when his presence is restored from following you, his goodness and mercy will cease to follow you

"For they got not the land in possession by their sword,
Neither did their own arm save them,
But thy right hand and thine arm, and the light
Of thy countenance, because thou hadst a favour unto them".
Psalm 44:3

When God hides his face from you, supernatural favour will cease to follow you, and the absence of supernatural favour is the reason why many believers are held bound in the valley of frustrations, complicated financial problems, business failures and crisis.

Child of God, turn away from your sins and iniquities, for they are many, let your conscience that is dead towards the will of God be come to live to seek the righteousness of God, when that becomes your decision, you will discover that supernatural favour will be restore to speak in your life issues as a living sign.

2. **WHEN YOU LACK THE FEAR OF GOD:** When you choose that to walk in the fear of God, you have decided not to walk in the supernatural favour.

Supernatural favour is not a divine occurrence allowed to be the problem of those who are wicked, crooked, rebellion in their ways against God, rather it is a divine occurrence to God ordained to be the portion of men that has decided to walk in the path where the fear of God will be the camp and lights that holds their relationship with God.

"What man is he that feareth the LORD?
Him shall he teach in the way that he shall choose.
This soul shall dwell at ease, and his seed shall inherit the earth.
The secret of the Lord is with them that fear him,
And he will shew them his covenant".
Psalm 25:12-14

The fear of the Lord is what you need to keep supernatural favour as a sign in your life, and in your business. When you don't have any fear or reverence for God or his commandment even as a believer you will begin to suffer anti favour which is clear sign that the flow of supernatural favour without restriction and without oppositions.

"Thy word is lamp unto my feet,
And a light unto my path".

Psalm 119:105

The reasons why many believers are frustrated in this dispensation in the financial, economic, and business acknowledge of nations is not just because the government policies are bad, but because the people of God are not obeying the word of God and biblical principles in their life pursuit. Hearing the word of God cannot bless the hearers but the doers when you became a doer of God's word supernatural favour will become a daily experience, a regular testimony, and unrestricted miracles of your lifetime.

When you choose to ignore tithing covenant, you will discover that supernatural favour will be far away from you. Your rebellion against the tithing covenant is a sign that your are despising the success and prosperity of God's house, how can you walk in supernatural favour when the welfare of God's house is not your pleasure.

"For the Lord hath chosen Zion, he hath desired it for his habitation
This is my rest forever, here will I dwell;
For I have desired to
I will abundantly bless her provisions: I will satisfy her poor with bread

Psalm 132:13-5

You need to return back to tithing covenant, then supernatural favour will return back to you, you need to form the habit of taking pleasure in the welfare and prosperity of the house of God and you will see supernatural favour following you as a manifold works of God ordained to build you up in all your engagements.

3. **WHEN YOU DON'T HAVE A LARGE HEART FOR SEED SOWING:** There is a dimension of financial favour that you cannot, and can never experience as a believe until you come a seed sower with a large heart to give money to God liberally, generously, and in a huge amount.

   The reason why many believers are not walking in higher dimension of financial favour is because they have a small hand, and a small heart in giving to God. Many believers even though they are prayerful, righteous, and spiritual are not walking in the realities of higher level of financial favour because stingy, and selfish when it comes to group to God, and supporting the work of God.

"But this I say, they which soweth sparingly
Shall reap also sparingly, and he which soweth bountifully
Shall reap also bountifully"
2Corinthians 9:6

Child of God, enlarge your heart towards God, and have a large heat in sowing for there is a measure and dimension of seed sowing that is required to provoke the outpouring of supernatural favour in your finances, and upon your business. When you step into that dimension of seed sowing, you will discover that certain opportunities for elevation, and wealth creations will flow to you without you begging them to come your way.

4. **WHEN YOU REFUSE TO DELIGHT IN KINGDOM PROMOTION:** Kingdom promotion is the act of pursuing the prosperity of God's kingdom by dedicating your resources, and your money to God's work, good works that glorifies God, and honour the faith of the saints.

When you refuse to take delight in kingdom promotion, you will lack the evidence of supernatural favour, because the favour of God's kingdom is the inheritance of men of faith who dedicated their resources to the promotion of God's kingdom.

"Lay not up for yourselves treasures upon earth,
Where moth and rust doth corrupt,
And where thieves breakthrough and steal
But lay up yourself treasures in heaven,
Where neither moth and rust doth corrupt. And thieves do not breakthrough nor steal.
Matthew 6:19-20

Kingdom promotion is ordained with the power of the kingdom order of favour, when you choose to be a kingdom promoter, you have accepted to walk in the realities of supernatural favours, and favour will begin to win towards you without you praying for it, and without your seeking for it.

PURPOSE OF SUPERNATURAL FAVOUR

Supernatural favour is ordained with the purpose, and with a sign, and the purpose why God allows his favour to follow you is to establish his mighty works of salvation and deliverance in your life, and in your affairs, and there are as follows

1. **TO RAISE YOU UP BEYOND THE LIMITO OF YOUR FAMILY BACKGROUND:** Family background cannot be a barrier to your rising and to your financial prosperity when supernatural favour is at work in your life, which means that your financial property has no opposition when supernatural favour comes to play a role in your destiny.

   ***"He hath made his wonderful works
To be remembered, the Lord is gracious and
Full of compassion".***

   Psalm 111:4

   It does not matter how low, how ridicule and how shameful your family background right now, something good is going to come out of your life, because supernatural favour is ordained to make something extraordinary out of ordinary man.

2. **TO MAKE THE POOR MEN RICH:** The release of supernatural favour is ordained by God to eradicate your poverty, destroy your shame and reproach, and to terminate your beggary life.

   ***"He raised up the poor out o the dust,
And lifted the needy out of the dunghill".***

   Psalm 113:7

   You may be a poor man right now, but the good news is that God has sent forth his own kind of favour to make you rich. You are coming out of the valley of emptiness, to be in charge of wealth and riches.

3. **TO END SEVERE SUFFERING AND HARDSHIP:** The presence of supernatural favour is ordained to break the siege of severe suffering and hardship in your life, finances, and business.

Anywhere you see supernatural favour at work, money cannot be a problem in that place.Anywhere you see the flow of money in abundance as answer to the need of a man, just know that the favour of God has visited that man in a higher dimension.

Your suffering and hardship is ending today, your financial crises and struggle are broken like a siege this moment, because the favour of God has come to play a role in your welfare. A new experience shall be your portion in your quest for financial liberty and economic freedom hence forth.

4. **TO CREATE OPPORTUNITY FOR SUCCESS & PROSPERITY IN THE ECONOMY:** God is creating opportunity for your success and prosperity in the economy, if the economy is not favourable to others, it shall be favourable to you. God is creating a way out for you to succeed and prosper even in the bad economy for that is one of the signs that must follow you as a believer.

   Opportunity of upliftment, is coming to your endeavours again, your destiny helpers are already in a position to stir up things, and arrange events to happen in your favour because God's dimension of favour has been released to play a role in your survival, and in your welfare as a covenant child of God.

5. **TO END FAILURE, TENTION, DEPRIVATIONS IN YOUR LIFE:** When supernatural favour is at work in your life, it will terminate failures, tensions, and deprivation of blessings.

   It does not matter how many times that you have failed in your quest to achieve success, your failure has ended, stand up from that place you are lying down and try again for there is success in progress waiting to embrace you in a double fold.

6. **TO GIVE YOU ACCESS TO DIVINE ESTABLISHMENT AND SETTLEMENT:** The release of supernatural favour is allowed by God to grant you divine establishment and divine settlement.

   There are many failed dreams, failed visions, and failed business that God is giving a second change to experience success, and your own is among them. Supernatural favour is released in your direction at this moment to grant you success in the places that you have failed before, and it open doors for you in the places that doors has shut against you before, as you walk in this faith, and walk in the light of this revelation, the events of your life will take a new shape, and new direction and record a new testimony.

7. **TO ANNOUNCE YOUR DUE SEASON:** The release of supernatural favour is ordained to announce your due season to bring you into the manifold blessings of God, and your timing to encounter divine visitation.

   Child of God, by the virtue of God's kind of favour release as a sign to accompany you, I decree and declare that your time to touch financial prosperity, and change status financially and economically has come, and nothing can stop it from coming to pass.

   In anywhere that you seem to be forgotten by God, there is a divine remembrance for you, and in any place you seem to be forsaken by God, here is a divine approval ordained to make your person acceptable before men positioned in life to bless you.

   Friend, enter into your due season with faith, and with singing because there is a release of supernatural favour by God to build you up, and for this same reason, time and events of life are under the divine commandment not to withhold your financial blessing.

CHAPTER 19

OPENING THE REALMS OF POSSIBILITIES

God is the God of times and seasons, God is the God that controls the four winds of the earth, he is the Lord of the earth the ancient mountains are under his control.

For miracles to happen against the believe system of men in every dispensation, there is no realm of experience that needed to open for sons of men to walk in the fullness of God's promises.

For the supernatural to subdue the national to give the saints dominion over impossibilities in every dispensation there is a realm of reality that needed to open for the believers to have a new life experience in the unfolding of the miracles.

For biblical prophecies to have permanence, and dominion over the affairs of men, and in the affairs of saints, there is a realm that needed to open for the body for Christ.

Friends, we are in the days of God's omnipotent power, and the realms of possibilities is opening for the saints of God to walk in the reality of the promises of God in dimension, and it's fullness.

"By tremble things in righteousness will
Thou answer us, O God of our salvation,
Who art the confidence of all the ends of the earth,
And of them that are afar off upon the sea.
Psalm 65:5

There is a realm of encounter that God is opening for the saints of God in this generation, and in the realm some of the promises of God that looks as if it is impossible to be obtained in this time shall be the occurrences happening in the camp of the saints, and in the life of the believers as we wait for the Lord's coming.

Friends, the realm of possibilities is a realm where what seems impossible in your life are made possible by the hand of God. The realm of possibilities is a realm where the success prosperity, and breakthrough dimensions that appears to be impossible in occurrence are made possible to be life experiences of the redeemed in the hard times as a sign that will follow them:

"They have seen thy goings, O God, even the goings of my God, my king, in the sanctuary.
To him that rideth upon the heavens of heavens,
Which were of old, lo, he doth
Send out his voice, and that a mighty voice"
Psalms 68:24, 33

The realm of possibilities is a realm where God changes the experience of his people from negative experience to positive experiences, something is about to happen in your life, your negative life experience that seems to be a curse is broken today, for positive life experience is appointed to begin to happen in your life from today henceforth.

When the realm of possibilities is opened in your life, they shall be a sign and the signs are as follows:

1. Your believe system about God, and about life shall be changed, and shall be healed by God.
2. Limitations in destiny shall be broken and your destiny shall establish gloriously with honour attached to it.
3. Every oppositions to vision shall be humbled, and destroyed, in your vision to experience breakthrough in the pursuit of your life endeavours.
4. Unstable success and natural circumstances are destroyed for your to enter into unrestricted and unlimited dimension of success in your business, finance, and life issues.
5. Stubborn curses of life are being broken, and helplessness are being eradicated for you to move forward in life.
6. Unrealistic dreams and evil blockages are being humiliated and destroyed for the dreams of God's people to find realities.
7. Times and seasons are re-positioned to welcome supernatural activities in the activities of the saints in the economy of the nations.

Child of God, this signs shall follow you, and this experience shall be your testimonies because God is opening the realms of possibilities in your life, in your case, and in your affairs, and by the hand of God biblical prophecies and promises shall be confirmed miraculously in your life in the mighty name of Jesus Christ.

WHAT DOES IT MEAN TO OPEN SOMETHING?

It means to unlock something that was locked so that the flow of it that has seized will begin to flow to the people again.

It means to remove a blockage to give the people access to something precious that was closed and looked from functioning.

It is the act of making available what was ceased to the people to begin to enjoy it again as their own right and previledges.

Beloved, God is opening the realms of possibility, in your life,miracles has been ordered by the breakthrough power to spring up in your direction.

WHAT IS A REALM?

Realm simply means an area of activity, interest and knowledge that control the functions of the human race and a people in the physical world, or in the spirit world.

To a believe, a realm simply means a place where the invisible exist to control the visible and to connect the sons of men to what has not revealed before, neither has it been done before in the history of man or among the people of God.

"But as it is written, eye hath not seen, nor ear heard,
Neither have entered into the heart of man, the things which God hath prepared for them that
Love him.

1Corintians 2:9

There is a dimension of wealth and riches that the world has not seen before, that God is connecting the saints to the realm where it can be accessed in this dispensation. There is a dimension of treasures of God that is kept in the realm as a precious thing of God's kingdom among the nation that is ready to be revealed to the saints in our time.

WHAT IS POSSIBLITIES

Possibility simply means a chance to achieve something, and opportunity that makes certain things to happen, even when there are factors that suggest that they are not possible.

Possibility to a spiritual person simply means access given to an individual, a people and a particular generation to raise their heads above circumstances and limitations that frustrated their predecessors from utilizing their potentials in the time past.

Friend, God is opening the realm of possibilities for you in this generation, whatever that limited the potentials of the former generations in their quest for fulfillment shall pave a way for you.

1. Gift and talent will make a way for you.
2. Time is redeemed in your direction
3. Exploit will answer to you
4. Opportunity is sealed to obey you
5. Realms of destiny is opened for you
6. Men will be at your service to help you

The things that are not possible in your life before now, are being made possible. Impossibilities are under the Lord's commandment to obey your authority in all your life pursuit.

CHAPTER 20
GOD IS SIGNING MANY CHEQUE BOOKS HEAVEN IS AWARDING MANY CONTRACTS

Beloveth, God is signing many cheque books, heaven is awarding many contracts to many people in this generation.

What does it mean to sign a cheque book: It is means to release money for a job to be done, it means to approve a release unto you by the parties involved.

There are works that are ready to be done in the kingdom of God this end-time, and there are services that requires urgent attention for the gospel to raise it's bar to dominate the world, and God has approved a release of money from his bank to men who are prepared to do his job for him.

What does it mean to award a contract: It means to give somebody or someone a job, or work to be done under a written agreement, or under a certain rule and regulations on how the job will be done, and how the payment will be made.

Beloved, there are mysteries in the kingdom of God that the believers need to connect to in this end-time, and this mysteries has to do with the invisible treasures of God, that can flow in the lives of men to become a physical material possession that can be used physically as a material wealth.

When it comes to the realm where money is being controlled physically and invisibly, God is an authority in that realm, he can bring you into abundance of wealth physically, and he can bring you into his invisible treasures to tap into store house in heaven to have the flow money in your life as a grace.

UNDERSTANDING THE UNSERCHABLE RICHES OF GOD

The unsearchable riches of God is the manifold treasures of God, and riches of his kingdom, and precious things of the earth such that has not been revealed to any man, or to any generation.

"The heaven, even the heavens, are the LORD'S, but the earth Hath he given to the children of men

Psalm 115:16

The unsearchable riches of God are abundance of riches and wealth that are hidden in the higher mountains of the earth, and in the invisible places of the world such that no man has discovered, and such that is yet to be revealed to generation to come.

Beloveth, God is set to reveal his unsearchable riches to his contractors in the generation, men whom he has prepared, and have prepared themselves to work for god with money that he will give into their hands, are about to embark in the journey of discovery, because their cheque has been signed, and contracts has been awarded unto them to do the work of God.

"For thus saith the LORD of hosts, yet once,
It is a little while, and I will shake the heavens, and the earth,
And the sea and the dry land.
And I will shake the nations, and the desire of all nations shall come,
And I will fill this house with glory, saith the Lord
Of Hosts. The silver is mine and the gold is mine,
Saith the LORD of hosts. The glory of this latter house shall be greater
Than of the former, saith the LORD of hosts;
And in this place will I give peace, saith the LORD of hosts.

Haggai 1:6-9

Beloveth, God has penetrated world economy, and the economy of this nation, very soon there shall be a change to be in the favour of men who are divinely positioned to show forth the greatness and excellency of our God in using their resources to do the work of God.

Very soon, they shall be a change in the economy of Africa, for God has touched the circulation of money globally to be in the favour of Africa in this dispensation.

Silver and gold belong to God, there are parts of his riches, and his treasures that can only be revealed in this dispensation to sons of God who has prepared themselves to stand as kingdom contractors in the body of Christ this end-time.

WHO ARE THE KINGDOM CONTRACTORS

Kingdom contractors are the believers who has consecrated themselves and their resources to do God's work, they are men who has a decision to be useful to God with their money, resources, and possessions.

Kingdom contractors are men who has trained themselves and have prepared their heart to do the good works of God's kingdom with every resources that he will commit into their hands.

"For we are his workmanship, created in Christ Jesus unto goodworks, Which God hath before ordained that we should walk in it.

Ephesians 2:10

Kingdom contractors are men who has received the calling, and have made themselves available to work for God with their material wealth, and do the good works of his kingdom with their money.

Beloveth, God is bring many sons into glory, and sons in the kingdom of God are the saints who has re-positioned themselves to render service to the gospel of Jesus Christ with their treasures.

Sons in the kingdom of God are the believers who has trained their soul build the walls God's house, and do the work of the ministry with their money as their humble service unto the Lord.

"And they shall build the old waste,
They shall raise up the former desolations, and their shall repair the waste cities, the desolations of many generations. But ye shall be named the priests
Of the LORD, men shall call you the ministers of our God,
Ye shall eat the riches of the gentiles,
And in their glory shall ye boast yourselves".

Isaiah 61:4, 6

Kingdom contractors are the believers who will make a decision to make themselves available for God to use them to do his work, make yourself available for the list is still opened, put your name in the list of men that God will use in this dispensation to reveal the excellency of wealth and riches among the heathen through is manifold works ordained to promote the end-time gospel, and to build the end-time church.

God is signing a cheque book for many believers to come into the position of wealth and riches, and to do his work with it.

Heaven is awarding many contracts in his kingdom to many believers who have prepared their heart to become God's workman in a financial matter.

Child of God, men who are in this category are men whose time to touch financial blessings is ripe, heaven has repositioned them to have certain strange encounters with the following experience

1. **A WAY OUT IS OPENED FOR THEM:** For men whose names has enlisted as kingdom contractors in the body of Christ, there is a way out for them in every situation, it does not matter how complicated the events of their lives may be right now, the way maker has made a way out for their escape from the low life, and for their financial promotion to happen suddenly by the mysterious help of God.

2. **A DOOR IS OPENING FOR THEM:** If you have made a decision to be a kingdom contractor for God in this dispensation, there is a door opening for you, a gate is opening for you, an access is given to you right now to enter into opportunity that is not common to men, and to have access to money that has not been revealed to mortals.

   If doors are closed against you before, they are opening right now, if gates are locked against you before, they are opening, barriers are broken, boundaries and borders of nations are about to welcome you back with unusual favour.

3. **CHEQUES ARE BEEN SIGNED FOR THEM:** If you have made yourself available to join the fold of kingdom contractors, cheques are been signed for you now with the signeth ring of Christ. The invisible hand of God has signed this cheque for you, the hand of mortals, kings, rulers, and governors around the world shall surely sign a cheque for you to do you good in your business, it must surely come to pass.

4. **THE CONTRACTS ARE AWARDED TO YOU NOW:** When there is a work to be done, they shall be a release of money, God is giving you a job to do, and that job is to be a kingdom promoter, a ministry builder, and a gospel pillar with your resources.As you positioned yourself to start doing this right now with what you have, they shall be an overflow and a billion increase in our finances, and it must surely come to pass.

5. **THEY ARE SUPERNATURALLY QUALIFIED BY GOD:** When God said that a man is qualified in life, it means that the man has received a divine

approval and recommendation from God to have access to previledges that is not common to man.

Child of God, you are qualified by God at this moment to become what you cannot be because by the making of man, but by the making of God you are crossing over limitations of life, you are pass-over the boundaries of success, you shall be a limit breaker, and rise to become a frontliner in your endeavours from today.

Every mountain of success that you cannot climb before shall be humbled before you, the book of destinies are opened in the heavenlies, for your sake, many generations and thousands of names shall be blessed for your sake.

The future will begin to work in your favour from today, and dispensation prosperity is welcoming you as an achiever, as a celebrity, and as a global personality in the list of wealthy men and great men, kind that will be your portion as a man walked for God, and as a man who walked with God.

CHAPTER 21
IT SHALL BE LIKE A DREAM
IT IS A REALITY

When miracles tarry, it will be like the miraculous has faded away among the people of God, and when the natural seem to be defeating the expectations of people of God, it will look like the supernatural have host their power, capacity, and authority to impose changes upon the ugly situations of people of God, and men of faith.

Friend, the miraculous are about to invade your ugly situation with a sudden changes, it shall be like a dream in your life.

The supernatural are about to demonstrate their power to you in that severe poverty and hardship where you found yourself and it most surely be a reality.

"Happy is that people, that is in such a case,
Yea, happy is that people,
Whose God is LORD".

Psalm 144:15

Child of God, even in that your poverty, I want you to give God thanks, and let your mouth be filled with thanksgiving and sacrifices of praise because the impossible is about to turn to unimaginable miracles in your life.

Even in that situation where poverty, and lack is mocking you, friends and relatives seem to be far away from you because of how ridiculous that poverty has humiliated you, I want you to start singing a joyful song unto the Lord as you sacrifice of praise and thanksgiving unto the a dead expectations is about to made alive again in your situation in the hand of God.

"God's the Lord, which hath schewed us light,
Bind the sacrifices with cords,
Even unto the horns of altar"

Psalms 118:27

When heaven is about to make intercession for you in the situation that is beyond your control, what they need from you is your thanksgiving, and sacrifices of praises, for it is a biblical commandment for you to give God thanks in everything both in the moment of hardship, lack, poverty, and in suffering.

Child of God, there is an intercession going on the heavenlies on your behalf, Jesus Christ the high priest of the saints according to the book of Hebrew Chapter 8:1-3 has already-made an intercession for the disappearance of your poverty, for you better life and better days to became a reality.

It shall be like a dream, but it is your reality every glorious things that God has spoken concerning you that has not seen the light of the day, is about to become our daily life experience.

It shall be like dream, but is a reality, your dirty waters shall become a clean water, those ugly stories that people has known you with it for years is fading away in twinkle of eye.

It shall be like a dream, but it is a reality every glorious things that God has spoken concerning you that has not seen the light of the day, is about be become your daily life experience.

It shall be like a dream, but it is a reality, your dirty waters shall become a clean waters, those ugly stories that people has known you with it for yours fading away in twinkle of eye.

It shall be like a dream, but it is a reality your dry land shall be made a watered land, anywhere you have been disconnected from your world, your future, and your dream life, there shall be re-connection in the spirit realm, and in the physical realm, things will fall in places for you in your personal affairs.

"Behold, the former things are come to pass,
And new things do I declare,
Before they spring forth I tell you of them".
Isaiah 42:9

The former and present things in your life that is not pleasant is fading away, and their fading away shall be like a dream.

God has vowed to release you into the realm of the new life experience, God has vowed to touch dreams and visions that are fading away in your life. God has vowed to touch hopes and future that is dead in your life and it must surely be your reality.

THE CLOUD OF THE PROPHETIC IS FILLED WITH BURNING FLAMES

The cloud of the prophetic is filled with burning flames and this burning flames are ordained to initiate a movement of change, in the affairs of the church, and the saints of God in this dispensation.

Child of God, welcome into the cloud of the prophetic, welcome into the burning flames ordained to destroy suddenly financial mockery and ugly experiences of your life.

Welcome into the era of change, because they shall be occurrences of sudden change in your financial matters, this change cannot be hidden, it cannot be slow, it cannot happen in unnoticeable way, it shall be an open testimonies for you.

"When the LORD turned again the captivity of Zion,
we were like them that dream
Then was our mouth filled with laughter, and our tongue with singing,
Then said they among the heathen, the LORD hath done great things for them".

Psalm 126:1-2

This change that is coming from above is bringing a change of position for you; the position you found yourself right now is above to change for you to move into a new position that will guarantee your financial liberty.

This change that is coming from heaven is burning like a flame, it is going to bring you into a change of life experiences.Every bad experience that you are going through right now shall fade away for a better experience to set in into your life.

There shall be a change of status for you, they shall be changed of fate for you, occurrences of your life is about to take a different shape, new frequency, and a new direction.

There shall be a change of situation for you, life is about to treat you with fairness, and with good things. There shall be a change of level for you, God is moving you into new places in life, where opportunities for better life will not turn their back on you.

They shall be a change of path for you, you are about to walk in the path where the rich, the wealthy, the noble, and kings of the earth are ordained by the virtue of birth right to walk.

"The LORD God is my strength, and he will make my feet like hinds feet, And he will make me to walk upon mine high places".
Habakkuk 3:19

There shall be a change in your economic welfare, grace is your portion, that grace is about to speak for you. They shall be turn around, in your standard of life, favour is your portion, that favour is about to be established to grow in an ever increasing way to meet your needs in amazing way.

REALITIES OF AMAZING GRACE

Amazing grace is the dimension of God's grace that makes ugly situations beautiful in a miraculous way, it is the aspect of God's grace that turns things around for good in your hopeless situations.

This amazing grace is restored with fullness of it's potency, power, and realities to effect changes in your financial crisis, and in your unpleasant circumstances.

When the amazing grace of God is that work in your life things cannot remain the same, they must be a unique and outstanding changes in your affairs to prove the miraculous has stepped into your life.

When the amazing grace of God is at work in your life, there is a dimension of divine acceleration and elevation that will be happening in your life to confirm that the supernatural has come to establish a living testimony in your ugly stories.

Child of God, there is a release of amazing grace of God into your life, into your situations, and into your finances, what shall be the outcome of it? Shall be the following:

1. **YOU SHALL JUMP OVER**
   One of the signs that will follow you from today is the grace to jump over, you will rise up from your paralysed state of life, and from your crawling life experience to jump over to a new world of financial liberty,

a new realm of sufficiency, and new phase of financial status where you will discover that all the road blocks, and evil blockages arranged to stop you, they are fading away with their heads bowed down in shame.

2. **YOU SHALL RUN FASTER**

You are waking up from your slumber to walk again into success, your speed is changing now, your frequency of movement in the realm of prosperity is taking a new shape. There's a place for you in the top, there is a place for you among the rich and the noble, your legs are strengthened today by the most-high God. Join the company of great achievers, great leaders, whose exploit in creating wealth in the world is speaking for itself.

When they begin to talk about men with economic power, money power, and investment power, your name shall not be missing in the list that is your inheritance in the written will of Christ.

3. **YOU SHALL GROW RAPIDLY AND RISE SUDDENLY**

Growing rapidly is the sign that will follow you from today, the yoke of stagnancy, badluck, delay, and hindrances is broken in your life, and in your finances.

There shall be a sudden rising for you in the world of business your growth is redeemed by the precious blood of Jesus Christ not to be held captive, and not to be in bondage.

You are rising suddenly to control money, you will be growing rapidly to control resources, God ordained you to be a believer that will be great achiever, a goal setter, and goal getter.

From today every natural obstacles that made you a man with unrealistic vision unrealistic future, and unrealistic glory is fading away for the new you to come into the picture and have a clear reflection in the affair of men that will give glory to God.

4. **YOU SHALL RAISE YOUR HEAD ABOVE LIMITATIONS**

There is a deliverance for your head, your head cannot remain in the company of ordinary men, low life men, and frustrated men.

God is bringing a lifting up, and upliftment for your head to wear a crown of glory, honour and praise among the achievers on earth, you are joining the company of men that subdued money, and made money their slave as a life time achievement, your poverty is fading away because God has chosen you to raise your head above limitations of life, the grace that empowers men to become what they cannot be by themselves, is coming upon you by the making of God.

Something is living your life today, and that thing is limitations, something is fading away in your head today that thing is a low life.

Child of God, something is disappearing from your life today that thing is poverty, the time for you to locate your place among the privileged people in the world, and among the favoured believers has come, and that must surely be your reality.

5. **YOU SHALL SOAR LIKE THE EAGLE IN THE SKY**

There are people whose sky s their limits, and there are people who are ordained by God with wings to soar in the realm of outstanding achievement above the sky.

I pray for you that you shall soar like the eagle in the sky, and soar like an eagle above the sky, the realms of achievement is opening from you, and the doors of global achievement is opening for you, it is your destiny to step into that dimension of glory and reputation, nothing can stop you.

The new dispensation of grace has come, it has unfolded itself, it has circulated in the cloud of the saints. It is announcing its presence in the atmosphere of the saints for the elevation of the covenant people of God and for the church of Jesus Christ to take a new height in the global economy for a fulfillment of prophecy.

Your name has been selected to tap into the grace of God for this dispensation, to walk in the realm where money will hear your voice and obey, where money will see you and bow.

CHAPTER 22

PRAYER WORKS FINANCIAL MIRACLES

Prayer is the key that opens every door including financial doors, which simply that prayers can do financial miracles in your life.

Financial miracles are miracles that has to do with supernatural provision of wealth and riches, prosperity, success and supplies of money in abundance in such that money to meet a needy is not a problem.

Financial miracles is the acts of the miraculous that commands and order money to locate you in the moment of needs, and before the need arises to give you the right of ownership over money in your daily needs.

Financial miracles is one of the strange works of God that can be provoked through your complete devotions to prayers in your walk with God.

"Blessed s the man whom thou choosest, and causest to
Approach unto thee that he may dwell
In thy courts, we shall be satisfied with the goodness of thy house,
Even of thy holy temple.

Psalm 65:4

God is a miracle work, God is the author of inancial miracles, and financial miracles is the heritage of the saints in the era.

Child of god, financial miracles is all about money provisions that funds your projects, destiny, needs, budgets, welfare, and survival with giving any room for you to struggle because of money.

When the needs arises, and money opposes great challenge to your survival as a Christian, and to your destiny as a believer what you need is the occurance of financial miracles.

When the needs arise, and money opposes great challenge to your survival as a Christian, and destiny as a believer what you need is the occurrence of financial miracles. By the grace God, may I inform you that prayers of prosperity, and petitions for material blessing is one of the prayers that God cannot turns his face on, neither can he turn his back on such a request in the midst of his people.

"For the LORD God is a sun and shield, the LORD
Will give grace and glory, no good thing will he withhold from them
That walk uprightly.

Psalm 84:11

Supplications for financial miracles is ordain for supernatural empowerment of the saints, and every supernatural empowerment is a sign ordain by God to follow the ministry of the prophets.

The ministry of the prophets is ordain carry financial miracle as a sign, and the mysteries of the prophets are ordain to carry supernatural empowerment as a sign.

By the virtue of this understanding, it means that financial miracles is a sign that follow you through the ministry of the prophets, when you begin to act on the prophetic.

"Believe in the LORD your God, so shall
Ye be established
Believe his prophets, so shall ye prosper"

2Chronicle 20:20b

Acting on the prophetic is the key to activate the supernatural, and obeying the instructions of the prophet is the key to command the miraculous.

Child of God, prayer works financial miracles is ordained by God to be a prophetic instructions that will lunch you into the realm of financial miracles to your total obedience to my instructions as a prophet of God.

70 PRAYER POINTS FOR FINANCIAL MIRACLES ENLIGHTENMENT

This 70 prayer points are anointed by the Holy Ghost to create and do financial miracles in your life, destiny, business, and dreams. You have to pray this 70 prayer points as a medium to connect to the flow of financial miracles that God want to recreate to you through your acts of obedient to this prophetic instructions.

Friend, as you put the prophetic to test with your obedience, you have committed the God of the prophetic to open the realm of financial miracles for you has an encounter even in this hardtimes.

There are signs ordain to follow this 70 prayer points as you prayer it one by one as the spirit of God leads, you miracles will begin to unfold it's in your directions in your finances according to your expectations, and beyond your imaginations in the mighty name of Jesus Christ.

70 PRAYER POINTS LINE-UP

1. The mysteries of the prophets be brought back in our days with financial miracles in the name of Jesus Christ.
2. The realm of prophetic encounter be opened unto me with a new dimension of financial miracles in the name of Jesus Christ.
3. The power of old that does supernatural miracles in the life of believers appear in my finances in the name of Jesus Christ.
4. The movement of God with a financial blessings locate my life, and my contact address in the name of Jesus Christ.
5. Demons in charge of poverty be arrested in my life, and be destroyed in my life in the name of Jess Christ.
6. Life afflictions in my life that came to stay in my have as result of poverty be terminated by the hand of God in the name of Jesus Christ.
7. Its donations organised to donate poverty to my life and destiny backfire in the name of Jesus Christ.
8. Monitoring spirits in assignment to withheld my encounter with financial blessings be arrested, and roasted by fire in the name of Jesus Christ.
9. Hands laid upon my head in the secret from the spirit of ordain my destiny with poverty be cut off by fire, expire in my life in Jesus name.
10. Incantations of diabolical powers made in the covens of darkness to hijack my wealth and riches in the spirit realm never to see the light of the day expire by fire in the name of Jesus Christ.
11. The seals of financial slavery be broken in my life in the mighty name of Jesus Christ.
12. The ancient financial bandage sealed by occultic powers with my dream life be broken in my life in the mighty name of Jesus.

13. Dream realms riches and wealth that has not seen the light of the day in my life, cease to appear in my dream life, and let my prosperity become a reality in the name of Jesus Christ.
14. Prophecies of riches and wealth that is delaying in my life, be hasted by the fire, and let the Holy Ghost bring it to pass in my life in the name of Jesus Christ.
15. Satanic empowerment ordained to block financial blessings of God to cease to flow in my life, catch fire in the name of Jesus Christ.
16. Covens of wickedness that has swallowed riches, and treasures in my life, vomit it by fire, and die by fire in the name of Jesus Christ.
17. Covens of witches and wizards in the upper surface of the earth ordained to destroy my financial prosperity, be destroyed by fire in the mighty name of Jesus Christ.
18. Covens of idols, and gods of my land that ceased and caged my star of riches and wealth, be broken by fire in the might name of Jesus Christ.
19. Covens of diabolical powers in my father's with a mandate to make me poor, be destroyed by the Holy Ghost in the name of Jesus Christ.
20. The gods of my village and community that has stolen my business progress and achievement, be destroyed by the Holy Ghost in the mighty name of Jesus Christ.
21. Every engrafted demons living in my life point of breakthrough be destroy by fire in the name of Jesus Christ.
22. Every exit mirror assigned to be an agent of enchantment against my days of breakthrough, be broken by fire in the name of Jesus Christ.
23. By the power of the Holy Spirit, I break away from financial circles and empty pockets in the name of Jesus Christ.
24. Powers assigned to employ my bank account through financial crisis, be arrested by the Holy Ghost in the name of Jesus Christ.
25. Series of occultic gang-up signed in the invisible realms to destroy my financial testimonies in Christ, be scattered by fire in the name of Jesus Christ.
26. Series of satanic attachment attached to my life to destroy my glory in Christ, catch fire in the name of Jesus Christ.
27. Evil attachment of poverty assigned from the coven of diabolical powers to monitor my life, and progress, catch fire in the name of Jesus Christ.
28. Power of the most High God, restore my glory in business with prosperity in the name of Jesus Christ.

29. Powers that has swallowed my source of income, and livelihood, vomit it by fire in the name of Jesus Christ.
30. Powers that has swallowed y financial helpers never to locate me in this life, vomit them by fire in the name of Jesus Christ.
31. Evil baptism of agents of darkness upon my life ordained to hide my glory in business, be destroyed in the mighty name of Jesus Christ.
32. Powers from the streams and rivers assigned to monitor my appointed time of blessing to manipulate it, be destroyed by the Holy Ghost in the name of Jesus Christ.
33. Activities of the economy of my nation, locate me with unbelievable business breakthrough in the name of Jesus Christ.
34. Release of supernatural empowerment, flow with the signs of the miraculous in my finances in the might name of Jesus Christ.
35. God of appointed time, let my offering, and tithes come to your remembrance for my blessings to be released in the name of Jesus Christ.
36. Satanic attacks against the premises of God in my life, be scattered by the Holy Ghost in the name of Jesus Christ.
37. The promises of God for my life that is under the persecutions and affliction of the enemy be redeemed by the blood of the lamb in the name of Jesus Christ.
38. The realities of salvation appear like the rising sun in my life, and in my status in the name of Jesus Christ.
39. The power that raised Jesus Christ from the grave, raise your arms against the adversaries of my finances in the name of Jesus Christ.
40. The wind of glory that attracts fortune for the saints bring my restoration, recovery from financial failures in the name of Jesus Christ.
41. The ancient yokes of financial failure, frustrations, suffering, and calamities be broken in my life by the Holy Ghost anointing in the name of Jesus Christ.
42. The yokes of hereditary poverty be broken into pieces in my life, and fade away in the name of Jesus Christ.
43. The curses of ancestral powers upon my prosperity, and my future that is tormenting my finances, be broken by fire in the name of Jesus Christ.
44. The gathering of the wicked against my success, and prosperity be scattered by the Holy Ghost in the name of Jesus Christ.

45. The gathering of witches and wizards against my financial breakthrough, be scattered by fire in the name of Jesus Christ.
46. Any offering given in the coven of native doctors to destroy the labour of my hands, expire by fire in the name of Jesus Christ.
47. Every causes laid upon my star in business by my friends, and enemies of progress be broken by the Holy Ghost in the name of Jesus Christ.
48. Every curses of evil and diabolical women upon the works of my hands be broken in the name of Jesus Christ.
49. The curses of star gases and future interprets upon my quick and sudden prosperity be broken by fire in the name of Jesus Christ.
50. My quick and sudden prosperity appear as a covenant in my life, and be delivered from the attacks of the wicked in the name of Jesus Christ.
51. Voices from the ancient covenant of my father's house speaking against my testimonies of salvation be silenced by the Holy Ghost in the name of Jesus Christ.
52. Every evil pronouncement made against my business growth in the altars of dark men, and dark women, it shall not stand in the name of Jesus Christ.
53. The healing power of God rest upon my economy and heal my finances in the name of Jesus Christ.
54. The restoration power of God rest upon the works of my hands, and let my future in life be restored in the name of Jesus Christ.
55. The restoration power of God rest upon the works of my hands, and let my future in life be restoration in the name of Jesus Christ.
56. The economy of this nation be visited by the supernatural hand of God that turn things around in the name of Jesus Christ.
57. The economy of this nation be delivered by every gangup of wickedness, principalities and powers in the name of Jesus Christ.
58. Economic devourers of this nation be located with the wrath of God, and be destroyed by fire in the name of Jesus Christ.
59. The cloud of our economy as the saints of God in this nation be exempted from the negative occurrence of this world in the name of Jesus Christ.
60. The financial activities of my country turn around and work for my favour, in the mighty name of Jesus Christ.

61. Demons created with mission to hang around me to destroy my existence, and my glory, be destroyed with your creators in the name of Jesus Christ.
62. Angels of the living God appear in the cloud of my destiny and redeem my times and seasons for my divine visitation to take place in the name of Jesus.
63. The word of God arise and be confirmed in my Christian life, and in my inheritance as a believer in the name of Jesus Christ.
64. By the word of my testimonies, I overcome poverty, and low life in the mighty name of Jesus Christ.
65. By the word of faith, I overcome the forces of frustration in my journey of life in the name of Jesus Christ.
66. Money I cannot be your slave from today, because you are made to serve me according to the covenant in the name of Jesus Christ.
67. Money that answereth all things flow in abundance, with all sufficiency in my direction in the mighty name of Jesus Christ.
68. The mysteries of the supernatural empowerment be interpreted in my quest for prosperity from heaven in the name of Jesus Christ.
69. With the flow of thanksgiving, I declare, and decree that my position is changing financially in the name of Jesus Christ.
70. With the flow of thanksgiving I baptize myself by the Spirit of God into financial liberty and financial blessings as my reality in the mighty name of Jesus Christ.

Author

Pastor Kingsley Udoka Nwachukwu hails from Ebonyi State of Nigeria. He did his Primary Education and High School in Nigeria.

He is an anointed man of God called into the vineyard of God to preach the gospel in the office of a Pastor, Prophet, and Apostle.

He is a man of God that experienced many heavenly visions from God, where the Lord gave him the mandate to take the gospel of Jesus Christ to the whole world, preaching the message of new covenant to all flesh.

He attended a Seminary School in Accra Ghana, where he was awarded a Degree in Bible and Theology. He proceeded to the Campus U.S.A. Ministry where he was trained in the School of Evangelism to be a soldier of Christ in grass root evangelism.

The Quest for Spiritual enlightenment on outstanding leadership prompted him to attend Word of Faith Bible Institute (WOFBI) where he was trained on the ethics and practice of Godly leadership.

He is an ordained minister of the gospel with the laying on of the hands of presbyteries upon his head in the presence of many witnesses.

He is the pioneer of Anointed Prayer Point Network in Lagos Nigeria, a grass root prayer outreach that has blessed many people with Deliverance, Word of Prophecy, fruitful prayer ministration that has produce diverse kinds of miracles and testimonies.

www.ingramcontent.com/pod-product-compliance
Lightning Source LLC
LaVergne TN
LVHW060822170826
845678LV00010B/1877

* 9 7 8 9 7 8 7 9 2 4 4 2 6 *